MARC SLEEN

SAFARI

NEW ENGLISH LIBRARY
TIMES MIRROR

Contents

	TANZANIA	Mwanza; Grumeti; Serengeti; Sanaane Island
	KENYA	Masai-Mara; Tsavo; Aruba; Malindi; Lamu; Kilifi; Mombasa; Kilaguna; Athi; Limuru
January 1968	UGANDA	Kidepo
	KENYA	Baringo; Hannington; Marakwet
	TANZANIA	Moshi; Arusha; Usariver
Jan./Feb. 1969	KENYA; UGANDA	Semliki; Kipedo
Jan./Feb. 1970	KENYA	Camel Safari; Northern Frontier; Malindi; Kilifi
	TANZANIA	Momella
Feb./March 1971	UGANDA	Murchison;
	KENYA	Ntarakana; Samburu; Uaso Nyiro; Tiva;
May 1971	ZAIRE	Kinshasa; Zongo
Jan./Feb. 1972	KENYA	Tsavo; Naivasha; Talek; Masai-Mara
	TANZANIA	Ngorongoro
Jan./Feb. 1973	KENYA	Magadi; Natron; Nguruman; Sambu; Meru; Rojeweru; Marsabit
	TANZANIA	Serengeti; Grumeti
November 1973	RUANDA	Gisenyi
	ZAIRE	Bukavu; Nyarogongo; Kahuzi-Biega; Ngoma; Rwindi; Rutshuru; Lubero; Beni; Ruwenzori; Butembo; Ishango
February 1974	CHAD	N'Djamena
	CAMEROONS	Matakam; Mokolo; Rumsiki; Garoua; Kapsiki; Waza
October 1975	NATAL	Zululand; Ndumu; Mkuzi; Umfolozi; Msinga; Hluhluwe; Empangeni
February 1976	KENYA	Lake Bogoria; Tsavo; Ntarakana; Tiva; Yatta; Baringo; Aberdares
Jan./Feb. 1977	KENYA	Meru; Mugungu; Nakuru; Baringo; Sigur; Lodwar; Eliya; Ferguson's Gulf; Lake Turkana; Central Island; Saiwa
Nov./Dec. 1977	KENYA	Masai-Mara; Meru; Wajwero; Nakuru; Limuru
August 1978	KENYA	Narok; Masai-Mara; Talek; Naivasha; Nakuru; Aberdares
Nov./Dec. 1979	KENYA	Shaba; Masai-Mara; Nakuru; Naivasha; Lewa Dhowns; Isiolo; Samburu; Lake Jipe

Introduction

A good deal has changed since my first safari in Africa in 1962. Encouraged by my late compatriot, Armand Denis, who became an American citizen, and was so well known for his television series, I visited Serengeti in former Tanganika. It was a difficult trek through Kenya, with a trip around Kilimanjaro, along roads which at that time were not asphalted but consisted of compacted earth, or along dusty winding paths, at the end of which one looked like a red Indian when emerging from the car. I will always treasure the memory of my joy when reaching Seronera, where, as the only tourist, I was heartily welcomed by Ian and Lasse Allan. Together with Myles Turner and his wife Kay, who lived in neighbouring Banagi, they were the only whites in that part of the world. Seronera consisted of some five straw huts, bandas or 'roundavells' with self-service. We had bought our food supply in Arusha, a town some 240 miles (400 kilometres) away. Never will I forget that evening. We enjoyed a Swedish-style meal, offered by Lasse and Ian, after which Tor, their thirteen-year-old son, gave the last bottle of milk to Serona, the tame otter. I had a last nightcap, and was ready to go back into the night when Ian pulled my sleeve : 'Should you not take a torch?' 'No,' I answered, 'I'll be all right, it is only a hundred yards.' 'Well, you had better look,' said Ian, as with the strong beam from his powerful torch, he picked up the yellowy eyes of three enormous lions who had stretched out at ease between my hut and the hospitable house.

Since 1962 I have crossed East Africa in all directions; by land, water and air. With the Land-Rover I covered an average of 3,700 miles (6,000 kilometres) per safari, a total of about 62,140 miles (100,000 kilometres). I have zig-zagged through the air over Kenya, Tanzania and Uganda with sports planes, the best way of going from one place to another in Africa. Flying low over the plains, the savannahs, the steppes, the bush, the bundu – however you wish to call it – I have seen great changes during the last twenty years. Where there sometimes used to be enormous herds, many areas now seem to be 'shot out . Only when flying over the national parks can one spot occasional, isolated groups of animals.

This is one of the most painful conclusions to write in an introduction. The average tourist, even the best informed among them, returns home with the happy remark: 'Everything is fine; there are plenty of animals. We have seen elephants, lions, buffalo, hippopotami, antelopes, giraffes and even a rhinoceros!' However, they forget that these animals can practically be found only in the national parks, where they are presented to the tourist in the most efficient way. Outside the national parks it is becoming more and more difficult to find any wild animals at all.

Some of the animal species illustrated in this book, such as the rhinos or the elephants, could become 'the fossils of tomorrow'. Much has changed in Africa – open conflicts, wars, political teething troubles – sometimes the entire land is a boiling pot. Political re-divisions, border skirmishes and shooting with the most sophisticated weaponry threaten African wild life.

The love of nature, the hankering after the exotic: the tourist industry has conquered Africa. The safari-boom with its infrastructure has made tourism the leading foreign exchange earner in countries such as Kenya.

The Rutshuru Falls in the Virunga Mountains, East Zaire.

5

Modern civilisation knows no limits. In some ways, tourism is the only life-line that can save the remnants of the once so mighty African animal kingdom. Tourism brings foreign exchange. The hungry, protein-starved, vastly increasing population, living in countries with extremely accelerated developments, is beginning to realise that its wild life, its heritage, is not a source of food, neither *nyama mkubwa* nor *nyama kidogo* – large or small meat – but a heritage as important as European cathedrals. One can make new works of art, but can never create even one grain of corn, one insect, or one bird, let alone re-introduce one of the numerous animal species that have vanished from the face of the earth. With institutions such as the World Wild Life Fund and the will of many nature lovers, in Senegal, Kenya, Botswana, Tanzania, Zimbabwe, Namibia or Zaire as well as in South Africa, neither population explosion nor human egoism will destroy the heritage which should be preserved for ALL peoples of this world and posterity.

Let us repeat the words of the Frenchman Jean Dorst: 'Who stops loving animals, stops being human.'

SERONERA as it looked in 1962. A few roundavells – a bed and a chair, food you had to provide for yourself.

In gratitude I dedicate this book to the man who taught me all that it contains: the Scot Gordon B. Harvey, a charming and humorous man and a born naturalist.

Gordon was born in Kandy, Sri Lanka (formerly Ceylon), on 2nd August 1908. In 1928 he went to Kenya as an assistant on a coffee farm at Kiambu, later Limuru. In 1930 he joined the Kenyan government in the colonial audit department, and in 1953 and 1954 was at the Kenyan Game Department at Isiolo, Northern Frontier District. He went from there to the Coast Province in 1956. He was appointed Chief Park Warden, Serengeti National Park, Tanzania at the Ngorongoro Crater from 1956 to 1959; and from 1959 to 1964 he went to Serengeti Headquarters at Seronera. He resigned in 1964 and accepted a partnership in Karl Pollman and Gordon Harvey Wild Life Photographic Safaris. Retirement followed in 1973, and he now lives with his wife Edith, daughter of one of the first Europeans to settle in Kenya, in Limuru, not far from Nairobi.

To quote Gordon: 'My first safari client was Marlin Perkins, famous for his Wild Kingdom Television programmes. Soon after that I took out Marc Sleen, who was to become a very good friend of mine. I had the privilege of taking Marc on nine safaris, always a real pleasure as he is a brilliant photographer and artist as well as a most knowledgeable naturalist and ardent conservationist. With Marc it is always 'go – go – go' planning, preparing, laughing, taking occasional risks – never a dull moment! Even after my retirement I took Marc on four more safaris, I simply couldn't refuse such a friend!'

Gorillas

Pili-Pili, a pygmy less than five feet tall, was crawling in front of me. His tattered boots, probably cast off by a colonial soldier, would have been a couple of sizes too big for me and the leggings which, in imitation of a trooper, he wore around his trouser legs, definitely dated back to the First World War.

A khaki army coat, in an advanced state of decomposition and six sizes too large, reached nearly to the ground in a hazard that would constantly have tripped me, but Pili-Pili persevered. With amazing suppleness he climbed through and over the bushes, hacking away with his panga at anything which could delay our march. Rain was lashing down, drenching us from an afternoon downpour which deluges the mountain forests of Kahuzi Biega with monotonous regularity. To my horror I suddenly discovered beneath me, between the branches, a chasm. We were walking on top of bushes – ten feet (three metres) above the ground !

Like an automaton I had been following the *bambuti*, crawling over and under branches, ferns and tree trunks, clutching on either side at lianas or bamboo trunks lifting heavy, muddy boots carefully across obstacles. It was now three o'clock in the afternoon. Since eight in the morning I had been sliding, clambering and stumbling through this tortuous, misty-wet woodland at a height of approximately 7,500 feet (nearly 2,500 metres). This was the Kahuzi Biega forest at the border of Rwanda and Zaire in the eastern part of Kivu. Suddenly I slipped on the rotting leaves and instinctively my hand reached out to a tree, which shattered into pieces with a sharp explosion. Rolling quickly to one side, I avoided an abyss by a hair's breadth and slithered down for only a couple of yards, clutching frantically at the undergrowth as I went – my left hand grasping an enormous stinging nettle and my right hand smothered by numerous small, black, furiously biting forest ants.

But what was I seeking here ? Was I quite mad ? Such acrobatics were better suited to circus artists or commandos. How could nine pigmies, some with bare feet, heavily loaded with cameras, tripod, film and food on their heads – a long procession of crawling, clambering and silent little people – possibly follow us !

In my earliest youth I had been an avid reader of the books written by the famous German naturalist Brehm, in which he related in a romantic and highly spiced way, how gorillas would attack and tear to pieces everything and everybody crossing their path. 'Nothing is more alarming than the attack of a gorilla', wrote Paul du Chaillu, the first white man to encounter a gorilla in its natural habitat.

As far back as in 1962 I had penetrated deep into the Kayonzo forest in south-west Kigezi in Uganda, in my search for gorillas. I did meet the sokumutu, the chimpanzee, but never a gorilla.

In recent years the scientific observations of pioneers in the study of mountain gorillas, such as George Shaller and Diane Fossey, had in-

creasingly awakened in me the desire to encounter a *Gorilla Berengei Matschie*. Then, at the end of 1973, I received permission from Dr Jacques Verschuren, Director General of the National Parks of Zaire, to enter Kahuzi Biega to film the gorillas. The man who would take me there was Adrien Deschrijver, warden of Kahuzi.

This gorilla expert is a remarkable man, whose achievements are unique. In 1966 Deschrijver was charged with the protection of the mountain gorillas in the Kahuzi region, at that time not yet a National Park, for which status it would have to wait until 1970. Taking advantage of the disorder preceding the new regime, the man-apes were hunted down by pygmies with lances, dogs, nets and bows and arrows as recently as 1965. Pygmies relish gorilla meat. As, additionally, collectors and zoos pay exhorbitant prices for gorillas, it is not surprising that pygmies have specialised in the art of trapping these precious animals. Catching them is easy. Bassengies, the pygmies' non-barking dogs, track them down. Mother gorillas are killed with arrows and lances and the young are easily captured. In the village the baby animal is handed over to some negress with a newly born infant for suckling. After an adaptation period of some months, the young gorilla can be transferred to a zoo and be introduced to other forms of feeding, usually by bottle.

Deschrijver received personal permission from the President of the Republic of Zaire to shoot down without compunction any poacher caught in the Kahuzi forest. This is why, since 1972, not a single gorilla has been hunted or killed in Kahuzi. President Sese Mobutu declared that all mountain gorillas were the personal property of the state. He set the price of a *Berengei* at five million Belgian francs. If a European or an American zoo wishes to acquire a gorilla, then this sum must be paid in cash to the Republic of Zaire ! The mountain gorilla is second on the list of animal species in danger of extermination. There is another species of gorilla, smaller in stature and occurring more frequently in West Africa : the lowland gorilla.

If a few years ago the inhabitants of Bukavu (the capital of the tourist area Kivu) had been asked if there were any gorillas in the forests of Kahuzi Biega, approximately twenty-one miles (thirty-three kilometres) away, no answer would have been forthcoming. Yet, one has only to follow the asphalted main road from Bukavu to Kisangani and in less than an hour one enters Kahuzi, which has some 350 mountain gorillas in an area of about 230 square miles. How could one possibly count the number of gorillas in such an enormous area, bearing in mind their timidity ? By counting their nests. Every night the gorillas collect branches and twigs to build themselves a primitive bed : the young and females up in the trees, the older males at the foot owing to their greater weight. These fresh beds enable the explorers to carry out a census of the animals in a specific region.

Feeding place of the mountain gorrillas. If you find recently broken bamboo stumps with the marrow removed, you know you are on the right track.

Formerly, the gorillas were actively persecuted and threatened, but now, since their integrated protection, their number is increasing, from 150 in 1966 to approximately double this number. Here in Kahuzi Biega now live approximately 350 of the 5,000 to 15,000 mountain gorillas still remaining in Central Africa. The poachers, the hunting pygmies, have been eliminated – by turning them into wild-life protectors. The father of Pili-Pili, the tracker with whom I was now trying to keep pace, killed the father of Casimir; the leader of the gorilla group we were now tracking. It must be said, in mitigation, that the father of Casimir was responsible for the death of Pili-Pili's brother. One could call it a family feud between the pygmies and the gorillas. An age-old battle of existence between forest dwellers.

It would be too simple to assume that the 300 or so mountain gorillas living in the enormous wilderness of Kahuzi could be approached without precautions. So far only two groups of those animals could be approached. A group of approximately eighteen members under the leadership of Casimir – named by Deschrijver after Dr Michael Casimir – and a second group some twenty-two in number, headed by Mus-hamuka.

The best proof of the meticulous care taken by Adrien Deschrijver to gain the confidence of these animals is the fact that only as recently as 1971 did he succeed in taking a photograph of the group, after having entered the forest with his Batwas on almost daily excursions since 1966. There is only contact with these two groups. The others still shun men, disappearing like shadows at the least sign of danger. Until 1971 gorillas, especially mountain gorillas, had been extremely difficult to film. They are shy, they hide amongst the bushes and undergrowth, and they are black. The few film sequences of gorillas living in the wild which have been shown in cinemas were, in fact, of animals which had first been surrounded or captured with the aid of hundreds of hunters and subsequently released in enclosed areas for the filming. Thanks to Adrien Deschrijver I was now at the point of reaping the benefits of his years of work. That was why I was here. I, too, wanted contact with the rulers of these mountain forests.

Fortunately Pili-Pili had stopped. In frozen silence he stood listening, his head tilted, his ear to the wind, the eternal smile which cut his wrinkled face in two had vanished for the moment. Luckily, the rain had also stopped. When I wriggled my toes I felt the water squelching in my boots. Adrien, until then at the rear, now came forward.

Pili-Pili had got the scent of gorillas. Perhaps he had heard them in the distance, beating on their chests; perhaps it was the snapping of bamboo, perhaps their pungent smell. Nothing on earth would now tempt Pili-Pili to stay in the lead. Pygmies have an inborn fear of gorillas, and perhaps not without reason ! In the old days, when, driven by hunger, they went out to hunt the man-apes, they smoked hemp to get 'Dutch courage'. They still do that. Should we be surrounded by the enormous animals, they would crouch down at once in a group and light hemp cigarettes.

Adrien, previously full of witticisms and dry humor, became silent. A frown appeared on his forehead and he suddenly looked much older. He talked with his hands, a kind of sign language, behind his back. Then he disappeared into the bushes.

Already beforehand he had given me directives : to stop talking as soon as contact had been made; remain standing and to move only very slowly – in slow-motion. 'Doucement, doucement', said the citizen of Bruges, who after twenty-seven years in the Kongo had forgotten his native language. 'Especially : don't run away when a gorilla charges.'

12

Casimir, the silverback. Patriarch and undisputed leader of the man-ape group.

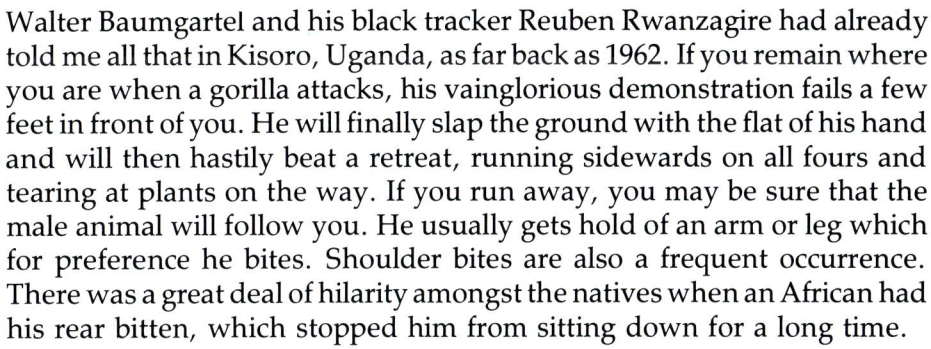

Walter Baumgartel and his black tracker Reuben Rwanzagire had already told me all that in Kisoro, Uganda, as far back as 1962. If you remain where you are when a gorilla attacks, his vainglorious demonstration fails a few feet in front of you. He will finally slap the ground with the flat of his hand and will then hastily beat a retreat, running sidewards on all fours and tearing at plants on the way. If you run away, you may be sure that the male animal will follow you. He usually gets hold of an arm or leg which for preference he bites. Shoulder bites are also a frequent occurrence. There was a great deal of hilarity amongst the natives when an African had his rear bitten, which stopped him from sitting down for a long time.

If you consider that an adult mountain gorilla can weigh up to 551 lbs or 39 stone 5 lbs (250 kilogrammes) – in captivity even 772 lbs or 55 stone 2 lbs (350 kilogrammes) – you realise that it is much better to keep calm and remain standing motionless. Remain still as if nothing concerns you. Personally, I find this the best solution. When a gorilla charges you – and I have seen it once – furiously beating his chest, his enormous pink muzzle with formidable jaws wide open, his hair standing upright and furiously swinging his huge arms – fleeing becomes impossible; you remain as if transfixed to the ground. You simple freeze in the midst of the African heat. Your heart stops beating for a moment. It is easy to understand that earlier explorers, such as Paul du Chaillu, at their first encounter emptied their gun into the hurtling monster. It has happened that older hunters suffered heart attacks and one young biologist when approaching the gorillas with Deschrijver fainted when Casimir charged.

Despite the fact that experience has shown that gorillas are normally good-natured creatures, great care is essential. A few weeks before his visit to the gorilla paradise, an African curator, who had taken a group of American tourists to the second group of gorillas, was charged by the leader, named Mushamuka. He caught hold of the African curator by a leg, swung him in a wide circle above his head and then threw him straight into the middle of the tourists – causing a great deal of commotion. Fortunately the assault resulted in only some bruises, cuts and a few broken cameras; unfortunately, no pictures were taken.

Yet, Deschrijver still goes unarmed. His only weapon is a razor-sharp pocket-knife, which he uses for efficiently cutting away branches and twiglets in order to obtain better visibility during filming. One of Deschrijver's set rules is that one must never approach the gorillas. *They* have to make the approach. Or at least one must give them the impression that they are doing that.

Without making a sound Deschrijver emerged from the dark undergrowth. He gave me a sign to follow slowly. Behind him I crawled on all fours underneath the lianas, through the dark bushes.

Reprovingly the citizen of Bruges looked at the nine heavily loaded pygmies, who, hardly silently, had penetrated the green tangle behind me. A

Tropical rain forests on the equator are fairly dark, humid and very hot; they are ideal surroundings for tree ferns (Cyathea) which can reach a height of 49 feet (15 metres).

bamboo trunk which had snapped in the middle appeared to occupy all their attention. It was filled with half-an-inch long (one centimetre) white larvae, which were eaten with relish by the pygmies. Probably it is a real delicacy to them !

We now entered a kind of glade, an opening with a visibility of some 33 feet (10 metres). Suddenly Adrien repeated the strange movement of the hand behind his back. He looked at me and his features had suddenly changed. His worry had been replaced by a relaxed and somewhat playful expression : 'Casimir', he said slowly, pointing in the direction of a dark hole some 30 feet (10 metres) in front of him. I could not see a thing; even when I carefully searched the area with my field-glasses. Adrien slowly went a few paces forward, halted and said; 'Come, come'. He broke, with slow movements, a young bamboo shoot, bit it, made a soft growling sound and said heavily; 'Casimir ... come, come'. And suddenly I saw in the bushes the black eyes light up. There was Casimir, the leader of the group of eighteen gorillas. The remarkable contact had again been made. Adrien had taken me to the gorillas. He only, with his group of carriers (and on occasion scientists or other interested people), is accepted by Casimir.

A kind of truce has been developed : an understanding. Most likely, Casimir accepts that there is another group – another kind of man-ape similar to him – and he tolerates that group coming to feed. He tolerates Adrien's group as non-hostile – a somewhat strange group, with sounds and smells he has come to recognise after so many years. American and English researchers of world-fame agreed this after years of study on the slopes of the Virunga mountain range. These timid rulers of the rain forests could only be approached with the greatest care and by preserving absolute silence. 'The only sound with immediate flight is the human voice', writes George B. Schaller, the greatest gorilla expert of our times, in his most recent work. Now here is suddenly a man who approaches the gorillas with a loud and in what seems to them an English voice saying 'Come, come, come ... ', Of course, they do not realise that these creatures painted until now as alarming monsters are addressed in West-Flemish by the man from Bruges.

Gorillas observe a well-considered daytime routine. They get up at about eight in the morning. Life is not hard. They find ample food around their sleeping quarters. With the exception of man and the leopard, they have no enemies. A leopard will shy from attacking an adult gorilla. Only young animals which have strayed away from the group are sometimes filched.

Besides feeding themselves with bamboo shoots, which they love, they also eat the stems of wild celery, ferns (marrattia) fruits and leaves of the musanga tree, myrianthus, fificus and even mountain nettles. As far as is known, they feed on 104 varieties of plants. Only when captured do they eat meat. Around midday they have their siesta and at about two o'clock in the afternoon feeding is resumed. At dusk, around six, the gorillas start making a nest.

At the end of the glade a strange scene suddenly awaited me. Casimir had slowly emerged from the dark undergrowth and stood now in the full light. Only the upper part of his body could be seen, but that was very impressive. His head, twice the size of a grown man's, towered above an enormous thorax. His sharp little eyes watched us piercingly from underneath the heavy, frowned eyebrows.

As I raised my camera slowly to my eye, a shrill cry burst out from behind me, which made my blood curdle. The cry came from the combined throats of the nine pygmies, who dived as one man at my feet, throwing their loads, packs, rucksacks and cameras away. Trembling and grey with fright they huddled together; a little heap of human misery. It all occurred so quickly. A few dull beats on a huge chest, which sounded to me like a war drum, and a deep growling made me realise what had happened. With one leap Deschrijver was between his pygmies and the bushes from which the loud growling emerged.

'Musharamina', he wispered in my ear as he passed by. 'A real racist ! Always attacks the pygmies in the back ! Cannot stand the smell of pygmies. Wants to be interesting !' Musharamina is the second in command of the Casimir-group.

The group accepts, entirely, the authority of the silver-backed leader, even though he does not seem to issue any orders. The group leader, usually the oldest and wisest, as always a silverback. He is thus called because the back hair becomes a silvery grey in ageing males. Gorillas do not live longer than thirty-five years.

There is always a set social order. Musharamina does not yet weigh the 441 pounds (200 kilogrammes) of Casimir, but he is well on the way to replacing Casimir, should the patriarch make room.

Then, almost unbelievably, Deschrijver made a few steps in the direction of the bush where Musharamina was hiding and said, raising a punishing finger; *'C'est fini, oui ! Du calme, du calme, voyons !'* Deschrijver here behaved as undisputed leader of the group. If he did not act in this way and if it became apparent during further contacts that he was a weakening leader, a dangerous precedent could be created, which would put the entire behaviour pattern and even the existence of the Deschrijver group at risk.

My camera was still at face level; but, when I directed my eyes to the place where Casimir had been sitting in the full light, he had gone.

During the following days we had several contacts with Casimir and his group. Sometimes it took six hours to reach them; on other occasions we tracked them down within a couple of hours. On one occasion we stood in a swampy bog and I filmed from there the gorillas above me in the trees; another time I filmed, from a fallen tree trunk, the feeding gorillas in a valley below me. *'Doucement, doucement,'* whispered Adrien to me on yet another occasion, when I was leaping from the one camera to the other. 'No nervous movements, you are too jumpy by far !'.

Two minutes later he himself was performing a kind of half-hearted Indian dance in slow-motion, scratching his legs furiously, searching in his trouserlegs for the *siafu* – the viciously biting inch-long (two centimetre) forest ants. We were right in the middle of them and would have to

remain there ! In front of us was Casimir in the shade of an enormous podocarpus tree watching our restrained but frantic war dances. To the right was Musharamina, living up to the pygmy name – after the recent attack on our bearers who were now sitting huddled anxiously together – and examining in lazy fashion the inside of a rotting hagenias trunk. To the left was a gorilla called Hannibal, slowly walking to a bamboo. He gripped the 4 inch (10 centimetre) thick trunk at a height of about six feet (nearly 1.80 metres) and broke it in two as if it was a match stick. With the same slow movements, he then took the trunk in his mouth, tore it apart with his teeth and ate the soft white marrow. Behind us, in the trees, I heard the sound of the feeding gorillas – the complete group – with once a glimpse of another black-back coming inquisitively to the edge; a young male, number four in the group, who later during my visit would be christened by Adrien Deschrijver with the suitable name of Nero. A gesture which I greatly appreciated !

On the last day Casimir suddenly approached me. To my left was Deschrijver. Tensely I filmed – concentrating only on the focusing and framing of my picture. I was worried that my camera might have been damaged by the brutal throwing down of my film material by the pygmies. Would these unique pictures succeed ? In my ears the revolving camera sounded like a diesel engine in a cathedral. Was Casimir disturbed by my proximity, did he see in me a new leader ? Was he irritated by the sound of the camera or was he just bad-tempered ? The fact was that he suddenly bared his teeth, uttered an ominous cry and, swinging his huge arms to right and left, rushed towards me. The tripod behind which I was hiding gave but little protection. I was so involved with my filming and things went so quickly, that I did not see what happened. With a sideward swing Casimir suddenly left me alone and paused on all-fours, his silver-grey back gleaming in the sun. Then, with a warning growl, he followed behind the entire troop which had already left the arena. Astounded, I looked down at the grass clods pulled out by Casimir which were now lying on my shoes. 'And what about this ?' said Adrien, pointing at his shirt which had been pulled out of his trousers ! As darkness was falling and no one was in the right mood to spend the night in the forest, Deschrijver gave the sign for us to start on the way back. With great relief the pygmies began the homeward journey. In a sudden and heavy downpour I once again tried to follow Pili-Pili, often sliding and stumbling over fallen tree trunks and lianas.

As he passed by, Pili-Pili cut down, with a firm swing, a tender banana leaf and put it on his head as protection from the gushing rain. In the early darkness we left the forest and I saw with unsuppressed joy the outline of the Land-Rover emerging from the edge of the road. I then realised that I had neither eaten nor drunk during the entire day. When I poured the sludge from my boots and soaking wet, steaming and dead-beat crawled into the car, I came to see the great fortune which had befallen me. I had been eye to eye with the ruler of the Central-African rain forest : the mountain gorilla. It was the most beautiful event in all my fourteen safaris !

Hopefully, good intention will succeed in saving these rulers of the Virunga mountain chain from extinction. Will people such as D. Fossey – who say that no mountain gorillas will be left in thirty years from now, if no drastic measures for their protection are taken – prove to be wrong ? It would be a shame if these splendid creatures, so near to us in the evolution theory, could only be seen in pictures and on films shot by some of us.

KAHUZI - BIEGA
ZAIRE 1973

Elephants

Herd of elephants in the Masai-Mara region at the border of Kenya and Tanzania; one of the few places in Africa where elephants have a chance of survival.

In my opinion, it is not the lion who is the king of all the animals, but the elephant. A lion makes room for the elephant. An elephant will not move *one* step out of the way of a lion. Has it not become apparent in recent investigations that the lion is a carrion eater ? That the hyenas hunt in troops during the night and have to give their prey to the lions ? During the day, when the tourists arrive, they find 'his majesty' on the killed prey. The cry then goes up : 'The king of the jungle has struck again.' That when the lion is only an indolent creature passing three-quarters of his life asleep, and content to let his females hunt to provide for him, not that we believe emancipation in the lion world to be necessary. No, it is the elephant who is the uncrowned king of the animal world; and he deserves to be, with his four to six tons in weight and his heart weighing 46 pounds (21 kilogrammes) and brains 11 pounds (5 kilogrammes).

Let us take a close look at his trunk for example. As a tool it is not less efficient than the human hand and that trunk has more than 40,000 small muscles, so an industrious investigator tells us. The trunk is really a very protruded upper lip with greatly extended nostrils; but the elephant can do all sorts of things with it. He can pull up a tree or pick up a small coin from the ground with it, as I have witnessed. Equally impressive is the fact that the elephant has his private ventilation system : his ears ! The enormous auricles guarantee the animal a fitting body temperature. By opening or closing the ear orifice, the elephant can allow or prevent warm or cold air entering.

It is said that elephants are noisy and ponderous. If they are shown in romanticised films or documentaries, their trumpeting can be heard for miles. This is not so in reality. Only when they feel completely safe, or when they are very close by, is it possible to hear the rumbling in their stomachs and observe their mutual signals. If it is necessary they can move practically inaudibly through the thickest vegetation without breaking a twiglet. Often I have found in the morning in the sand next to

How can man have the audacity to exterminate these wise, impressive and noble creatures, who, despite their ingenuity and superior force, threaten only in self-defence ?

my tent, and even between the guy-ropes of my tent, the imprints of their feet, without having heard them during the night. That fantastic capacity for stealth is due to the heavy legs with thick and supple calluses which absorb practically every sound.

Although elephants are by nature peaceful giants, some things make them very aggressive, such as toothache, for example. The colossal teeth, one on each side of the upper and lower jaws, change and this causes a lot of pain.

Doum palm (Hyphaene coriacea), *their fermented fallen nuts are considered a delicacy by elephants.*

Besides the frequently occurring toothache, drunkenness may also cause a great deal of trouble. Sometimes the animals eat the berries of the 'marula' tree or dropped and yeasted doum palm nuts. When they eat these they can become thoroughly intoxicated. Under the influence of Dutch courage, they are liable to be quite awkward with human beings.

A group of male elephants which I and Gordon met during an evening trip along the banks of the Uaso-Nyiro river (pronounced as Nero over here), showed clear signs of intoxication. With no indication of their usual timidity, they were leaning indifferently against the trees with crossed front legs, waving their trunks in a nonchalant manner to and fro, as if nothing interested them. Then one of the giants left his tree and with rather shaky knees approached our vehicle. Gordon quickly started the engine and we left the happy bunch. We were both thinking of the German tourist who had been taking pictures some months before of fruit-eating elephants. Only at the very last moment could he escape when one of the drunkards was on the verge of settling down on the bonnet of his V.W. As with human beings, intoxication can have disastrous consequences. These consequences are in direct proportion to size when an elephant is drunk !

Ivory
the white gold

In the old days the whole of Africa belonged to the elephants. The numbers of these impressive creatures (of which in the last century one and a half million roamed the black continent) have fallen in an alarming fashion. For example, in Uganda, where forty years ago they had seventy per cent of the country at their disposal, they now have to manage on twelve per cent. This decline, which can be observed over the entire African continent, is accelerated as man hunts them mercilessly and deprives them of more and more habitats.

When Sir Samuel Baker, the British explorer, followed the banks of the Nile in 1863, he observed, travelling parallel to his caravan, thousands of elephants spread over the plane for a stretch of 1 1/2 miles (2 1/2 kilometres). There were so many of them that he could only guess at their numbers.

Rennie Bere, the former director of the Ugandan National Parks, considers the number of elephants living in the Kabelaga and Ruwenzori national parks to be 15,000. Temple Perkins estimates the total number of elephants living in Uganda at 20,000. (After Amin Dada and the Tanzanian troops it will be less.)

The reason why this largest of all the world's land animals is hunted and being exterminated is not, as one might expect, to provide the starving

David Sheldrick, for years head of the Tsavo National Park, Kenya, here shows a heavy elephant's tusk. This white gold, taken from poachers, was stored in reinforced wharehouses. Every few weeks lorries would appear by order of 'the authorities' to remove it to Nairobi. In 1977, David Sheldrick was removed from his paradise to do administrative work in the capital. He died a few months later of a heart attack.

native population with his three tons of meat – but for something far more precious; something which he carries on his head : *IVORY*.

The high prices which ivory yields cause bands of poachers to enter the national parks and kill the elephants with sophisticated weaponry. To the slaughter must be added the effect of constant drought. In the period 1961-71 drought killed thousands of elephants. In 1970-71 I witnessed the catastrophic results of a thirteen months' drought in the East Tsavo region above the Galana River. More than six thousand elephants died during that time.
The research carried out by Timothy Corfield to find the reason for death showed that the majority of the dead animals were females and calves; the present and future propagators. As a result there will be a decline in the local elephant population over the next twenty years.

Heavy ivory such as this elephant drags along on his head, has become a rarity. Elephants no longer have a chance to reach old age and produce enormous tusks.

Because the elephants are being increasingly driven back into national parks there are serious problems. Formerly, when the whole of Africa belonged to the elephants there was a natural balance between flora and fauna. When one district had ceased to supply food, they went to another. This is no longer possible as the growing human population demands more and more land and the national parks become compounds inside which the elephants are imprisoned.
Dr Ian Douglas-Hamilton who studied the elephants for many years in the Tanzanian Manyara Park says that the elephants are being killed more rapidly than they can propagate. David Sheldrick, who died recently, told me himself that in twenty years' time there would be no elephants left in Kenya. Without doubt, within the next ten years the elephant can be on the verge of extinction if the trade in ivory is not drastically restricted. As elephants breed only every four years or more – the female is 660 days pregnant (nearly twenty-two months) – they may have vanished from many African countries such as Uganda, Kenya or Zaire in ten or twenty years. If there is no check on the sale of ivory there will be no stopping the fatal decline and man, who considers himself to be the crowning glory of animal evolution, will have succeeded in destroying the majestic noble elephant, the greatest animal in the world.

Tembo

We had called on a Liangulu tracker. They are known as the smartest elephant hunters, with amongst them definitely the highest number of ivory poachers in the world. They have it in their blood : from father to son, the hunter instinct has possessed them. No tribe in the whole of East Africa knows how to follow the track of an elephant better. We took our Land-Rover to within a few miles of the place indicated by the Liangulu, and there we left our vehicle in the shade of an enormous monkey-bread tree, the legendary baobab of which it is said that it can live 2,500 years and that it is amongst the oldest living things on earth. The baobab had in its trunk an opening which could easily accommodate five people.

Clearly, this was a hiding place for poachers. The large tip which I had promised the African made him decide to part with a few of his secrets. On foot and observing complete silence we proceeded at a slow pace; the semi-naked Liangulu, ex-elephant hunter Gordon and I, laden with cameras, heavy tripods hung like guns around my neck. It was nearly four o'clock in the afternoon, a heavy, sticky heat of around 85°F(30°C) in the typical desolate Tsavo landscape, in which a feature is the 'wait a bit' thorn bushes; and wait you must when you are hooked onto them. It is much easier to tear your complete sleeve out than to free yourself. The sharp hooks tear the skin from your legs if you forget to walk around these bushes in a wide circle. Don't expect straight lined progress in the Tsavo-bundu, unless you want to emerge like a wounded soldier.

A herd of elephants from the Sudan enters a scorched part of Kidepo National Park in north Uganda.

Suddenly the Liangulu stopped and pointed with an out-stretched arm to a *donga* or dried-up river-bed which rolled its way between two banks. At the end of it there was a watering place, a kind of pool. There, the Liangulu said, is the place where the elephants will come. We trusted him : Gordon is rather selective in the choice of his men. He had carefully checked and picked the best man of the tribe. The Liangulu pulled himself up into a shady tree. He was going to inform us, by imitating the 'go-away-bird', of the arrival of the elephants.

Together, Gordon and I climbed the bank. Some 300 yards (300 metres) farther on we discovered the pool. The water remained between the rocks in this watering place. According to the Liangulu the elephants come here every day at dusk to quench their thirst. In the dried-up river-bed we discovered footprints and droppings of the giants.

We opened the tripods and placed the cameras. Everything was prepared. The slightly sloping bank gave us a good view. We stood about two yards (two metres) above the river-bed. As soon as the tracker warned us we could put our cameras in motion. We would track them from the left to the right, following the herd to the watering place : Gordon in readiness for a British television programme, I for a Flemish one.

After three-quarters of an hour we were still there. I got cramp in one of my toes which I had struck, the previous year, on a coral reef in the Indian Ocean. Sweat was pouring from all our pores. Gordon stood like a statue; his Sherlock Holmes cap kept the sun out of his eyes and his trousers looked rather too full to be fashionable. No word was spoken. I only observed the twinkle in Gordon's eyes when I tried to moisten my cracked lips with my dry tongue. Bwana Beer, 'Mr Beer', his African helpers call

A baobab hollowed by elephants can be an excellant hiding-place for photographer.

The baobab or monkey-bread tree (Adansonia digitata). One of the oldest forms of life on earth. It is said to live as long as 2,500 years. It has a large trunk, with a circumference which can reach over 65 feet (20 metres) in old trees.

26

The hollow trunk of the baobab often contains a water reservoir. The spongy trunks of these gigantic trees contain, even during droughts, a surplus of water and calcium. The bark contains a substance (adansonine) *with fever-repressing properties. Elephants searching for moisture, penetrate deep into the trunk with their tusks.*

Poacher's baobob in east Tsavo. Some ten people can shelter with ease in its hollow trunk.

me. But the drink had to wait until our return to the Land-Rover.

Suddenly we heard the Liangulu's perfectly imitated cry of the bird … and there they were, the elephants – not in the river-bed but on the bank, their silhouettes contrasting sharply against the sky. The sun was low, evening was approaching; filming would still be possible but not for much longer. The cameras were already running. Thirsty, the great beasts, exhausted after a long day in the powder-dry Tsavo plain, marched in double-quick time to the drinking holes. Then a mother elephant followed by a baby, about 3 feet (1 metre) high, left the column and walked into the dried-out *donga*, straight towards us. Only then did we discover that, at our feet, was a hole into which the elephant put its trunk and began to suck up the water. The little elephant also dropped into the hole. Mama swung her trunk around her ears. Water and mud flew in all directions.

It was one of those small holes which the elephants dig in dried-up rivers. At a lower level there is always some water which will filter up. This was obviously the personal watering place of mama elephant and her toddler. With ears spread wide, the elephant stumbled down the bank to use the pool. In her hurry she had not even observed us and was entirely occupied by the water. However uneasy I felt (my back had turned stone-cold) the cameras continued to run. What would happen when the elephant discovered that in front of her on the bank were two miserable creatures with film cameras ? Just one step forward, one swing of her massive trunk would have finished us off. Who would be the first victim ? Gordon and I were standing shoulder to shoulder. I was sorry I was not behind Gordon, not for reasons of protection, but I could have taken superb shots of my Scot so close to a wild elephant. Oh ! If only I could show an elbow of Gordon or a piece of his head in my picture …

With the narrow-angle lens I was using I covered only the head of the elephant. The same shot could be made with the telephoto lens at a distance of 100 feet (30 metres). We had prepared to catch the elephants on their way to the river, to film their merry performances, the play-acting, their stamping about and bathing … now we stood eyeball-to-eyeball with the mother elephant. She suddenly froze; she had seen us. No more filming now. Petrified I looked on, transfixed, convinced that this was to be my end. The elephant spread her ears wide. She looked enormous. Then she made a step in our direction and placed herself between us and her baby. Well, there we go, I thought … two miniscule humans against the three-tonner. Softly the elephant turned, pushed her little one with her trunk in the direction of the main watering place and walked away with great dignity in her typical elastic gait.

My throat was cork dry, I could not talk, my moist hands gripped the steel of my tripod. No thoughts of filming were left in my brain. Gordon, the man who had shot over a hundred elephants when employed in the Game Department, when they were sick or uncontrollable, observed dryly : 'Never before quite so close to a wild elephant !' Gordon should know and that was really something. A quarter of an hour later, with legs still shaking, we were back in the Land-Rover and I had more than one beer to relieve my tension.

TSAVO, EAST KENYA

Unaware that we are near by, the mother elephant with her baby makes her way to her favourite drinking-hole.

Greedily the water is sucked up from the little pool.

Suddenly the mother elephant stiffens. She has seen us.

Totally ignoring us, the elephant turns around and goes back to the herd.

Gordon Harvey and a ranger with a record specimen which died not far from our Tiva camp (1971). The animal had tusks weighing about 190 pounds (87 kilogrammes). Poachers had no chance to steal the ivory, which had a value of approximately 300,000 Belgian francs.

The great drought

Not only the old but also young animals die as a result of drought. If the mother elephant cannot find enough green fodder, of which she devours some 550-660 pounds (250-300 kilogrammes) a day, she will not have enough milk for her baby.

Thanks to their trunk and tusks, which they use skilfully as tools, elephants can dig holes in dry river-beds and extract ground water from a depth of up to four and a half feet. Many other animals, such as rhinoceroses and antelopes, can survive a drought because of these small holes. In emergencies we, too, used the sand-filtered water to meet our requirements in camp. In any case, drinking-water was so precious that we did not waste it on washing-up or shower-baths.

Tsavo

The Tsavo National Park covers an enormous uninhabited region of more than 13,000 square miles (20,800 square kilometers) divided into two sections, east and west, by the main Nairobi-Mombassa road, which crosses it. The western part, with the well-known Kilaguni, Kitani, Ngulia and Salt Lick, is frequently visited by tourists.

The eastern part, north of the River Galana, is forbidden territory for tourists. Only with a special permit from the Game Department is this paradise open to them. Practically without roads, without water or facilities, one is entirely dependent on one's own initiative. It is an extremely dry, barren, hot, dusty, wild and, at times, impenetrable slice of real Africa, with at least sixty species of mammals and a bewildering profusion of over three hundred varieties of birds – a place where I had the good fortune to camp with Gordon at the Tiva or in Ntarakana.

The barrier between the 'passable' roads of the tourist route and the wilderness is the River Galana with its rapids, grotesque rock formations and the Lugard Falls forming insurmountable obstacles.

The Rivers Athi and Tsavo meet to form the Galana, which runs from here to the Indian Ocean.

Brief encounter between a lesser Kudu antelope and a rhinoceros, which has now become very rare, in the barren, sun-scorched Tsavo region.

pternistis leucoscepus

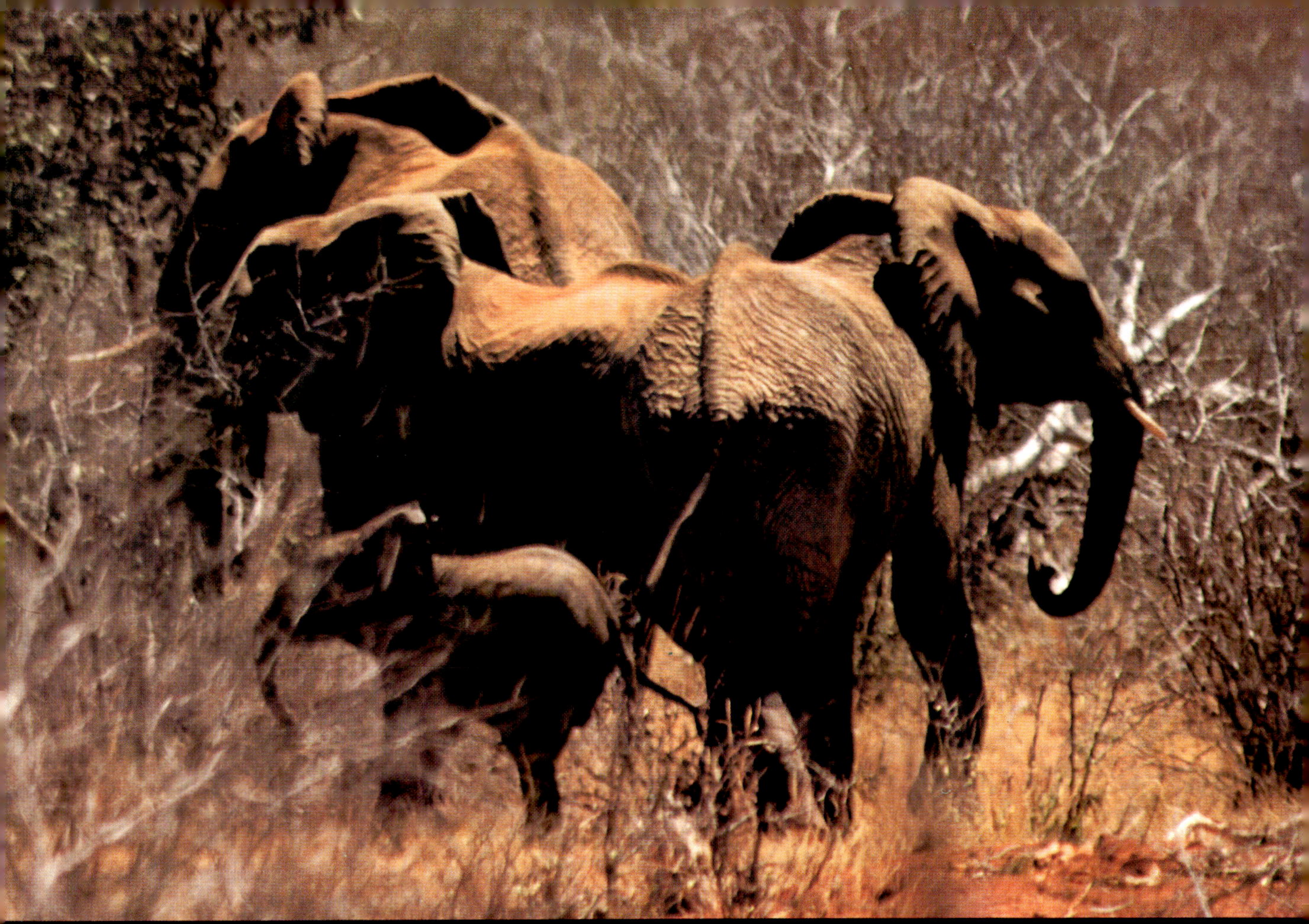

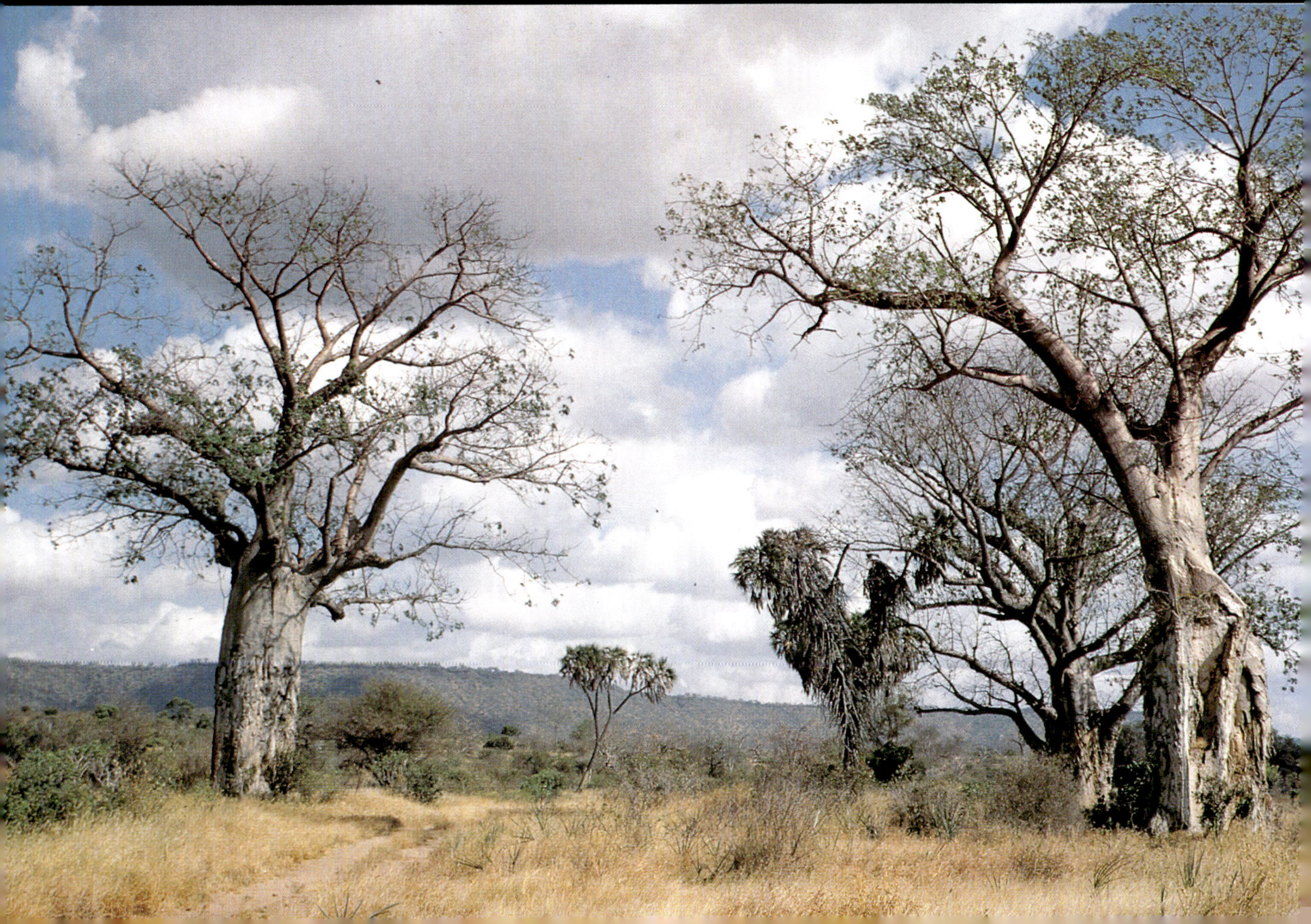

Everywhere that water is to be found, animals will be seen quenching their thirst.

The red earth

Termite mounds, sometimes enormous structures of Tsavo sub-soil that have been pushed up by the insects, prove (on this and previous pages) that the colour of the soil on which they live determines the colour of animals. The elephant and rhinoceros, which are fond of dust and mud-baths, come to look like redskins. BLACK rhino seems hardly the right word for an animal with such an appearance.

Mudanda rock – a natural hollow in the rocks between Voi and Manyani – contains, after the slight rains of November and December, a supply of water which attracts many parched animals, anxious to quench their thirst.

Rhinoceros
Requiem for a heavy-weight

Left and below
The black rhinoceros (Diceros bicornis), *in contrast to the white rhinoceros, is a partial grazer as well as a vegetarian nibbler. He uses his elongated upper lip to crop the most juicy shoots of acacia bushes and also eats grass. He is very fastidious over his food.*

For many millions of years the rhinoceros has lived on our planet, inhabiting an area from the South Pole to the Malay Archipelago, and from Java to South Africa. Now only five species exist of which a mere three hundred of the Sumatran species are left. They are irrevocably dying out, due to man's greed and his pre-occupation with sex. As long ago as 1513, the Indian rhinoceros was brought to Lisbon, Portugal. Albrecht Dürer based a famous woodcut on one. In the nineteenth century the Javanese rhinoceros was practically extinct. In 1978 in Nepal I had the good fortune to watch the last remaining animals out of about a thousand Great Indian rhinos. So man, all of 4,000,000,000 strong, and at the top of the evolutionary order, has succeeded in less than two hundred years in almost causing the extinction of an animal that has been on earth for so many millions of years.

The two African species have outlasted the eastern varieties, perhaps because the inner parts of the African continent were discovered by the white man only during the nineteenth century. Until 1812 it was thought that there was only one species of rhinoceros in Africa, the black or prehensile-lipped rhinoceros. Then, when he had rounded the Cape, the naturalist William Burchell discovered another variety south of the Zambesi, the broad-lipped rhino. The Boers, when exploring South Africa, gave the animal the name : *weidliprenoster, weid* pronounced as wide, but meaning 'broad'. The English, hearing this, misunderstood and misnamed the animal 'white rhino' or 'white rhinoceros'. There was some reason, for the rhino takes his colour from the dust he loves to roll in, or the mudbaths he adores. That dust or mud can give him either a white or

Right
The rare, white, or square-lipped, rhinoceros (Ceratotherium simum) *is more a grazer who crops the grass like a cow. His weight may be over 3 1/2 tons, he has a kind of humpback and is much larger than the black rhino. The cows, whose pregnancy lasts seventeen or eighteen months, give birth only every three years, and the young ones stay from five to seven months with the mother. What appears sometimes to be a couple, becomes mother and offspring on closer inspection. A peculiarity is that the black rhino mother walks in front of her offspring, while the white rhino mother trots behind her baby.*

red colour, depending on the area he happens to roam in; red in Tsavo, white in the lava soil of the Ngorongoro crater in Tanzania, black in the mud of the Aberdare mountains.

In the twenties – years I will never forget – there were only about twenty white rhinos left in the whole of South Africa. A massive rescue operation was launched in Natal, where in the meantime the National Parks had been established. The stringent protection was such that once again the white rhino came to be seen in other parts of Africa. But the white rhinos have quite disappeared from the Upper Nile and Chad regions, which they inhabited for so long. According to the expert K. Curry-Lindahl, the number of rhinos in the National Garamba Park (the only place in the enormous country of Zaire where the white rhino can still be found) had dropped from a thousand to about a hundred between the years 1963 and 1966. This represents a drop of some ninety per cent based on the figures of 1966.

Rhinos are greatly threatened by the shrinking of their habitat. Their limited adaptability also plays an important part in the reduction of their numbers. They can live only in an area with a strictly equable environment, and if they are driven out of their area, then it is extremely difficult for them to find a suitable new place to live.

The temperament of the prehensile-lipped black rhinoceros is totally different from that of the placid white rhino. The white giant can be approached on foot without the slightest danger, but care must be taken when approaching the unpredictable, quick-tempered black rhino. Their sense of smell and hearing are very acute, but their sight is poor. Strangely, at birth and during youth the rhino has excellent eyesight, but his sight weakens rapidly as he becomes older. When the beast is five years old, he can no longer see at a distance of fifty-four yards (fifty metres).

This poor eyesight, temperament, aggressive nature and the vicious horn on his head, have all made life very complicated for the three-ton animal. He has no chance against the modern weapons of the hunters. Even though there is a hunting ban in Kenya, poachers succeed in penetrating

According to the Pesident of Kenya, Daniel arap Moi, the rhinos will vanish completely from his country if drastic measures are not taken.

Jaw bones of elephants and rhinos, collected for study by scientists, are bleaching in the sun in the Tsavo plain. All were victims of poachers and the great drought.

The charge of Faru, *the rhino. The horn (which is not real horn) is composed of hair, and is not an integral part of the skull or bone structure. It is a kind of growth, a fibrous protuberance consisting of keratin (derived from the* Greek *keras keratos, horn), which is impervious to water and rich in sulphur. Keratin is also the fundamental basis of nails, hooves, hair, feathers, and so on. The horn may break – as Gordon Harvey experienced when he was subject to a frontal attack from a rhino. Faru landed with his horn between the front bumper and radiator of Gordon's vehicle. The shock made him lose not only consciousness but also his horn. He fell on his side, but after some thirty seconds he rose uncertainly and staggered weakly, but with dignity, into the bushes, leaving his horn on the battlefield.*

An expert approaching a male rhino can make him appear from the bushes without difficulty by imitating the sounds of a female on heat, or the cries, usually in minor key, of a rival. With raised ears and nostrils the rhino will come into the open to investigate. Bear in mind to place your vehicle in such a way that you can escape quickly in the event of a charge. Remember also that you are not parked on an asphalt road, and that Faru can spin around on his axis and is much more mobile than you might imagine.

the National Parks to obtain the precious horns. The reputed physical effect of rhino-horn rests on legend and this legend is causing the extinction of a species at the top of the World Wildlife Fund's list of endangered species. The belief that the hornpowder of the rhino stimulates sexual desire is quite unfounded, and the powder has no aphrodisiac value whatever. However, for centuries, rich Chinese, Indians and Arabs have kept the illusion alive. The mating of the rhino in an act which lasts longer than thirty minutes has caused horn to become a legendary and powerful phallic symbol with secret and especially stimulating powers. An intensive trade and ever-increasing prices have been the inevitable result of this persistent legend. Ground rhino-horn is still sold in Chinese chemist shops – where it is still also possible to buy dragon's teeth and other exotic articles to be found in myths and folk tales. John A. Hunter, the man who claims to have shot more rhinos than anyone else (over a thousand, but all by order of the government), made a brew of rhino hornpowder and drank it. So did the famous Dr A. Schaurte, who tested the brew scientifically. The results were negative. Yet, despite all protective measures some two thousand kilogrammes of rhino hornpowder were imported into South Yemen during the first quarter of 1977.

I have personally witnessed the enormous decline in rhino stock over the years. Whereas, in 1962, with, or without Gordon, I frequently came across black rhinos in east or west Tsavo, this colossal animal is now becoming increasingly scarce. Only in the National Parks, and with strict supervision, is it possible for these creatures to survive. Elsewhere commercial interests and wars have brought the animal to the verge of extinction, as in Angola, Chad, Uganda, Zaire and Mozambique. Serious conservators have suggested removing the horns from all rhinos in Kenya in order to protect their existence. I doubt whether this would prove to be the solution, as a sawn-off horn would grow again. The only way to save the rhino is to transport him to the National Parks. Experts such as Ian Player in Umfolozi, Nick Carter in Kenya since 1963, and Dr John King do their best to save those that are still left.

On the flanks of these white rhinos in Zululand one can see clearly a multitude of parasites, especially ticks. The glossy-starling in the foreground is no help but a tick bird would know what to do to rid the animals of their tormentors.

Symbiosis?
Feathered friends

And indeed that is what the tick birds or ox-peckers can rightly be called. They live on parasites and climb like miniature woodpeckers onto both wild and domestic animals and inspect the skin for ticks and maggots. One is tempted to speak of 'symbiosis' in connection with this very special bird. However, 'symbiosis' only applies to animals or plants which have become so interdependent that their chance of survival is interlinked. In the case of tick birds, we may call them most welcome liberators who relieve their hosts of awkward insects, but both bird and rhino can survive without this co-operation.

There are two species : the yellow-billed ox-pecker *(Buphagus africanus)* and the red-billed ox-pecker *(Buphagus erythrorhynchus)*. Although they belong to the starling family, they differ on account of their special broad beak, their short legs with the middle toe considerably shorter than the outside ones – a rarity for birds – and the stiff, pointed tail. Ox-peckers are true benefactors. Large animals such as the rhinoceros and giraffe are only too pleased to have the tiresome ticks plucked away from their ears and nostrils.

Not only do these birds free their hosts from annoying insects, which frequently transmit disease, they are also excellent guards : they give warning when there is danger for their host. Many a hunter or poacher has seen his trophy vanish at speed, even when appoaching his prey against the wind, alarmed by the flight of the birds from his back. Ox-peckers are found both on domestic animals – in Uganda I counted a record of nine on a small goat (photo right) – as well as on giraffes, rhinos, buffaloes and gazelles.

Hippopotami

'Hippopotamus' comes from two Greek words – *hippos*, a horse and *potamos*, a river; hence the name 'African river-horse'. Why these two-tonners have been called man's most noble conquest, remains a riddle to me. Formerly, they were frequently seen along the Nile, right into Egypt, where they appeared thousands of years ago in the hieroglyphics on the tombs of the Egyptian Pharaohs and where they infuriated the farmers by trampling their crops at night. Now they are found only in the upper regions of the Nile, the Sudan and beyond. If you are really keen on seeing elephants, go to Tsavo in Kenya or the Luangwa valley in Zambia. You will encounter crocodiles in the former Murchison, now the Kabalega National Park, or on and around the Central Island in Lake Turkana. Even in broad daylight it is possible to meet hyenas in the Ngorongoro Crater in Tanzania, and white rhinos in Hluhluwe (pronounced Slusluway), Natal and Zululand. As for the hippos, there are two places in Africa where they can be found in large numbers, or schools : Rutshuru and Semliki in Zaire, where some 15,000 live together and in Kabalega, Uganda, where there are also quite a large number.

Hippos give the impression, quite wrongly, of being cumbersome and unwieldy. Although they have the appearance of overgrown pigs, their bodies contain hardly any fat at all but muscles, rich in protein. Their habits also do them injustice. They are nocturnal animals, passing the day asleep and dreaming lazily in the water, because of their skin, which is very though and sensitive to heat. The South African Boers made their formidable sjambok whips of it, which they used during their treks to spur on the ox wagon teams.

Owing to their massive consumption of grass during the night, which they spread as manure in the water, they have a far-reaching influence on the ecology of rivers and lakes. Hippos have the longest intestine of all mammals, longer even than that of the elephant, and complete with

Ishango, the Garden of Eden at Lake Mobuto in Zaire, is one of the best places to study hippos in Africa. The mother animal, right, has three pied kingfishers on the look-out. She, herself, protects her very young baby. Birth and suckling the young take place under water.

fourteen stomach sections. Lakes and rivers where hippos live are usually well stocked with fish.

Whereas they give the impression of being cumbersome and placid, with their enormous bodies and short legs, they can move quite quickly if necessary. The best demonstration of this is to be seen when startled hippos run to their favourite hiding place, water – the time when they are most dangerous. Hippos always use the same routes in and out of the water, and form deep trenches which can be man-high, and inside which there is no vegetation. Should you happen to be on one of these paths, especially in the early morning or late at night, then the frightened beast will run at speed down his track to the water. The result of such a meeting is more serious than a few broken ribs or a ruptured liver. In the cemeteries of Uganda there are more graves of people accidentally killed by hippos than by elephants and lions put together. Never venture into a hippo's ditch during the evening or even in bright moonlight, and do not think that hippos are dangerous only when frightened and met on their paths to a river. Care is essential in the water as well. The older males, well aware of their superiority and male leader's duties, may charge. Heaven help the canoe or small boat which has to sustain an onslaught from the two-ton monster, or an attack from a muzzle filled with vicious fangs.

Hippos quietly dozing in the Mara River in Kenya. Old 'fighters' are sometimes completely covered in scars.

During one of my later safaris, in August 1978, I saw what such a charge could mean. Tor Allan, who accompanied me on that safari, had caught a large catfish at the junction of the Mara and Talek Rivers. He had gone knee-deep into the water to rinse the fish after having cleaned it. A bull, from a group of some ten hippos, left the group and raced with enormous speed towards him. Had Tor been in deeper water, he would not have

lived to tell the tale. David Lockwood, whom I accompanied on a canoe safari on the Tana River in north Kenya, had an ingenious way of keeping pugnacious and bad-tempered hippos at bay. As soon as he spotted a hostile bull's head rising with a great shower of foam out of the water, he reached not for his gun, which was kept near at hand for protection, but for an enormous horn, as used in long-distance buses. He placed that horn at the front of the canoe's bows in the water and sounded it. All zest for further attack or any show of aggression disappeared immediately. Ian Ross, at the time chief park warden in the Kidepo National Park in Uganda, in the top corner of the border with the Sudan, had an enormous hooter. When elephants entered his little private garden in the middle of the night to flatten his melons or papayas, he – with or without pyjamas – would race' outside to blow his horn. In 1965, when I was staying at his home, I was scared stiff, when in the middle of the night, I heard that hellish racket just outside my open window. You get used to the noise of thousands of cicadas, crickets, night swallows and frogs, with, in the distance, the vanishing hyena howling, but definitely not to the sudden blowing of a London double-decker bus horn near by ! The next morning Ian apologised, when he showed me, at the breakfast table, the musical instrument which had a permanent place on his bedside table. He also showed me the devastation in his miniature vegetable garden where there was no end of damage, as if a troop of soldiers had performed their drill there. 'Oh, well, they will stay away for a few nights now' said Ian calmly.

Quite apart from the show-off hippos, one of them once nearly caused me a heart attack. I was camping, together with a young Rhodesian on Musaradona-Spurwing Island, a small island in Lake Kariba in Rhodesia (now Zimbabwe) near the border with Zambia. In his small motor boat we set out each morning to film water birds in the small creeks overgrown

A lone two-tonner on a stroll in the Semliki plain (Uganda). At night they sometimes cover up to 3 miles (5 kilometres) grazing in the surrounding plains.

A bad-tempered male hippo, threateningly showing the forward pointing incisors of the lower jaw. During the mating season, the males are especially aggressive.

with papyrus, which was a birds' paradise : large and small white herons, squaccos, malachite kingfishers, cormorants and purple herons. In the rising sun I filmed the jaccanas, walking with their long blue toes on the waterlillies, carefully lifting the leaves to pick away the little slugs underneath, or the pied-kingfishers, who shot like torpedoes into the water, after having hovered overhead for a long time. All was peaceful and quiet. The sun was not yet burning, there was only the muffled cry of some lake-coot, or the far scream of a fish eagle answering his cousin on the far bank of the lake, or the soft amorous whispering of a reed warbler in a nearby creek.

Then suddenly to my right, a small distance away from my elbow, appeared the enormous head of a hippo. My heart stopped beating at the sight of the monster. Only afterwards did I realise that the hippo, walking along the bottom as they do, was equally frightened when he appeared at the surface and saw me. I still don't know who was more scared. After all, it is the fright reaction which counts most. One recalls stories of wild hippos swimming underneath boats and lifting them high into the air, throwing everybody on board into the water. In some tales, Africans have been bitten in half in the process. Such horrific tales can be heard everywhere in Africa. The hungry population is only too quick to inform the 'game department' responsible for the wild-life stock, when, during the night, elephants or hippos damage their crops and they demand the punishment of the culprit. It is understandable too, when natives have seen a year's agricultural work destroyed in one night, to blame a lonely thick skin for the offence. After all, a shot elephant or hippo divided on the spot amongst the local population will fill many empty stomachs. During one of my numerous stays at Michael Skinner's at the heavenly Baringo Lake, the tale went round that a cow had been bitten in half by a hippo. The local responsible authority, since Africanisation an African, was informed and the decision was taken to punish the culprit. The punitive expedition consisted of the 'game ranger', a sharp shooter, two helpers, a boatsman and I, who had received very special permission to film this brave mission. At the time, there were only nine hippos alive in the mighty Baringo Lake, that stretched for miles in the African rift valley. Yet, that most dangerous animal, who had bitten a cow in half, would have to be killed, although a monster which attacks cows would not hesitate to send humans to the hereafter. However, we were off. In front, his gun ready, was the sharp shooter. Quietly the long motor boat slid out of the reeds, all the helpers on the look-out across the smooth glassy surface of the browny-grey Baringo water. The natives knew precisely the place where the group congregated. They constantly talked about *Kiboko kali*. *Kali* is evil, angry; *Kiboko* is Swahili for hippo. The sun was burning, there was no breeze to cool us. Suddenly an outstretched arm went up. The accompanying Njemp had seen the group. They have fantastic eyesight, these chaps. They can see a couple of hippo eyes breaking the surface from a great distance. I spotted them with my field-glasses only when we were much closer.

A wide-opened muzzle is a clear threat not to come closer. Some African travellers think this 'yawning' is only a sign of boredom or laziness. In zoos hippos go 'begging yawning', but that is another matter altogether.

Slowly we approached. Inquisitively, a number of heads appeared, one after another; I counted nine. But how were we going to identify the culprit ? The engine stopped. The wrongdoer would be punished. After all, he was *kali*, the evil eye. Heads went down and with a great splash came up again, and the eyes looked inquiringly around.

We were now about 100 feet (30 metres) away. The two parties studied each other. The hippos appeared to be peace-loving gentle creatures, coming ashore at night and frightening only a few of thousands of goats with their enormous mouths and threatening attitude. (These goats roam the once beautiful land around Baringo Lake and are turning it into a desert.) No, they did not appear to be dangerous to me at all. As far back as in 1965, I would go into the water and merrily swim amongst them, both along the banks and in the middle of the gigantic lake. At the time, and even now, the lake is still inhabited by crocodiles and hippos. The late David Roberts, who died of a mysterious illness, his sons and the very young daughters of Michael Skinner, swam daily in the cool brown water of the lake. We believed that the numerous crocodiles and hippos did not attack us because there were so many tilapia (a common fish) that they were no longer interested in human flesh. As for the hippos, David Roberts explained, the cause of misbehaviour is always based on their strong and well-developed territorial instinct. It is not necessary to splash around in the middle of their well-defined area or in the centre of their group. Along the extensive banks of the Baringo Lake, the hippos can be found in well-defined spots and they spread out only during the night. The fact that the hippos are good-natured here is proved by Jonathan Leaky, who has a snake farm and melon nursery at Baringo. I knew that Jonathan gave many a tame animal the run of his garden, yet I was surprised when, a few years ago, I encountered a baby hippo there. The thick skin was sleeping in a kennel. Every morning, after her breakfast consisting of a large brown loaf, she walked contentedly down to the lake and every night when called by her name, Suzy, she returned to her doghouse. To me these giants belong in the splendid Baringo Lake and when I take a swim in the tepid water of this heavenly lake, I always feel at a distance the gaze of the friendly giants – as if they are saying : 'Are you enjoying it, too, today ?' Never did the thought enter my mind that these equable giants could be dangerous.

Alan Root will not support this statement, I am sure. When he, and his wife, Joan, and cameraman, Martin Bell, were taking underwater pictures of the hippos in the crystal-clear water of the Mzima Springs in west

Hippos in Nile lettuce, or weed, (Pistia stratioides). Although they make channels through rampant weed, they do not eat it. Their main food remains grass, of which they consume some 440 to 660 pounds (200-300 kilogrammes) a night. It is difficult to believe that their intestinal canal nearly 55 feet (some 17 metres) long, can cope with such a quantity of food.

Tsavo, armed with aqua lungs and underwater film cameras, they approached the animals in their most private territory ... and he was attacked by an infuriated male and dispatched to hospital. His wife was simply thrown out of the water, but Alan had some nasty bites on his legs and his foot and ankle were more or less mangled. An Italian doctor, who witnessed the event, rendered first aid, after which a tourist plane took the unfortunate camera operator as quickly as possible from the Kilaguni Lodge to Nairobi. As, besides all his injuries, Alan Root developed gangrene as well, his life was in the balance – not for the first time, because a poisonous snake had once bitten his thumb, causing it to be amputated ! According to Allan Root, hippos are top-scorer man-killers of all the grass-eating mammals in Africa; coming next after the crocodile who is carnivorous. However, I maintain that hippos, if left alone, and bearing in mind their territorial awareness, are good-natured animals. I just cannot imagine Lake Baringo without the nightly concert of hippos. Not so long ago (what, after all, are a hundred years ?) elephants and lions, leopards and thousands of antelopes wandered through this very beautiful region : now it is barren, stripped clean by hordes of goats and emaciated cows.

Mzima Springs, the crystal-clear water springs in West Tsavo. In this oasis, surrounded by acacias, yellow-fever trees and numerous palm trees, some 49,500 million gallons (2,250 million litres) of water emerge daily from the dry lava soil. It is a good place to watch hippos, crocodiles and other animals.

In this heavenly spot the famous animal film maker Alan Root was attacked by a hippo and injured.

So, when the game warden cocked his gun and pulled the trigger, I closed my eyes and refused to film. Great confusion on all sides indicated that he had missed with his first shot. Eight minutes later an enormous head reappeared some 65 feet (about 20 metres) behind the boat. With great speed the FN gun was raised. The Africans found it difficult to forgive the fact that at that very moment I got a very bad bout of coughing, complete with an apologetic gesture. White men are no good in black Africa... Later I learned that, in the greatest secrecy and without interference of white man, the cow-killer had been punished.

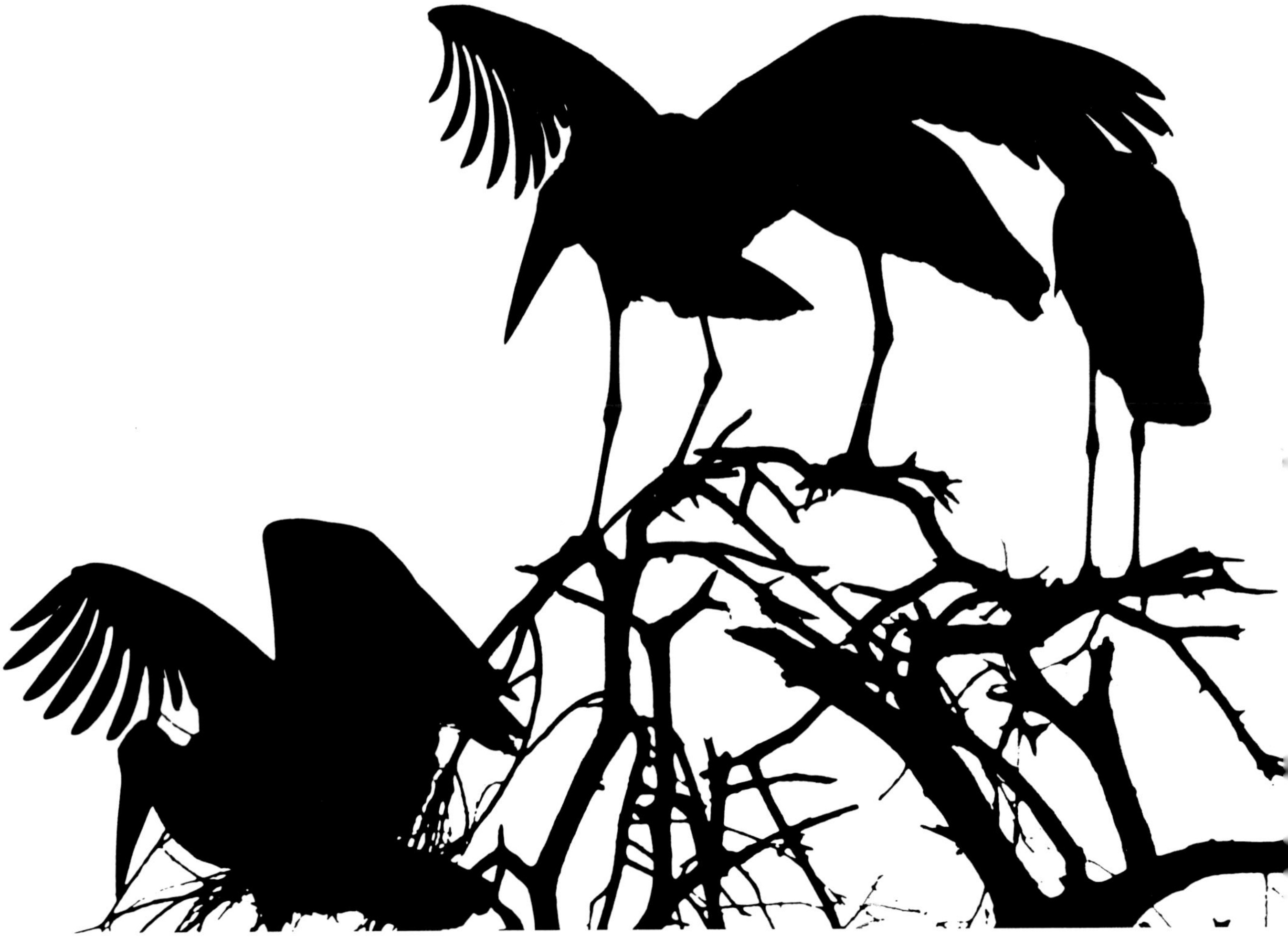

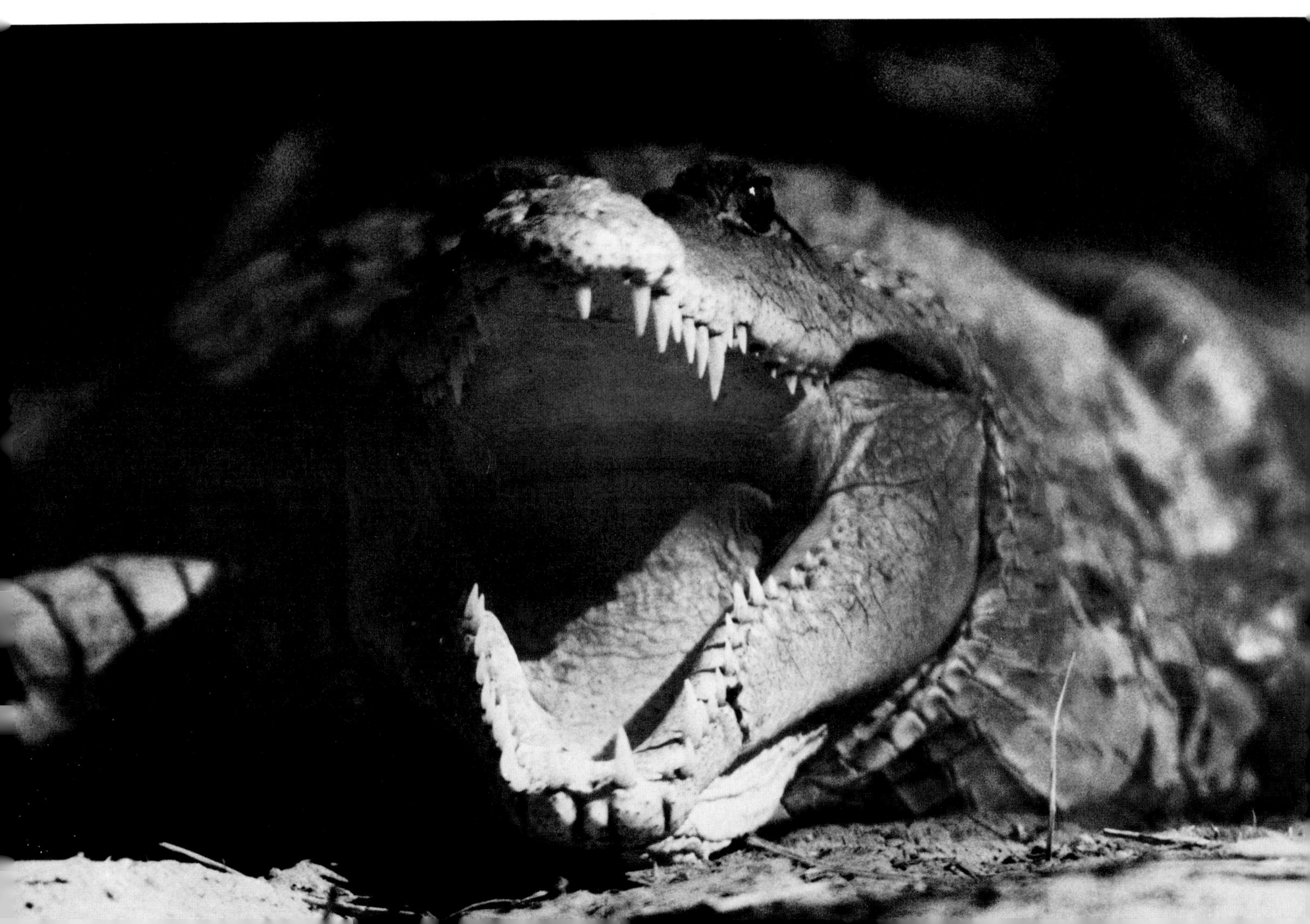

Baringo

Less than a hundred years ago, in 1887, Count Samuel Teleki von Szek, a Hungarian explorer and geographer, in search of the Jade Sea which he would later rename Lake Rudolf, discovered the heavenly Lake Baringo which became a halt for all caravans coming after him, where they could obtain their supplies. Less than twenty years ago, in 1963, when I visited this splendid area for the first time, one could not enter it without a special permit. In Nakuru, the Provincial Commissioner's Office issued a pass which was essential for gaining access to Mogotio or Marigat. The Great Rift – a 5,800 miles (9,000 kilometres) long fissure extending from Arabia to Mozambique – was caused by violent subterranean shocks which cracked the earth's crust and caused volcanic eruptions and fissures. This is the site of a ribbon of lakes, which we discuss in this book : among them Turkana, Baringo, Bogorria, Nakuru, Naivasha, Magadi, Natron, and Manyara. Some of them are alkaline. The strange phenomenon of Lake Baringo is that the water remains fresh, yet it borders the more southern Bogaria (formerly Hannington), Nakuru and Elmenteita Lakes which are soda-salt. There is also no visible outlet through which the minerals can escape. Scientists say that at one time Lake Baringo was connected to Lake Turkana by a river. It is possible that this connection still exists but is now underground. The sub-soil of the lake consists of volcanic ash and ancient porous lava strata, which absorb the water like a sponge

In this sun-scorched region, hemmed in by a towering steep dam of black broken lava, one imagines oneself in another world. This large water surface, over 10 miles (17 kilometres) long with numerous small islands, has always held a strong fascination for me. I have returned on many occasions. After Naivasha and Nakuru it is one of the most important bird paradises in Africa which, fortunately, is overlooked by tourists owing to its location and the absence of large game. Each small island is a natural El Dorado. The largest breeding-place for the goliath herons in East Africa can be found on Gibraltar Island, and cormorants, African darters and night herons breed here. More than three hundred species of birds can be studied in peace.

The largest island, Ol Kokwe, is the home and harbour of the Njemp fishermen, who mainly keep goats but also some cows. On the East bank of the Ol Kokwe are hot water springs containing sodium carbonate; springs hot enough to boil an egg, a sign that subterranean forces are still active, changing the landscape of Africa. The natives – the Tugen and Njemps – avoid these places, which they consider to be sacred.

The other islands – Parmorak, Langcharo, Samatian – are really unspoilt slices of nature. Samatian, with its rock formations and luxurious vegetation, is impenetrable.

Lake Baringo is rich in fish : especially tilapia, a kind of perch, which is caught in huge quantities. A member of the Njemp tribe can be seen in the lake up to his waist in the water, fishing peacefully for tilapia, while crocodiles on the same mission swim by. Natives go fishing with an ambach, a special canoe or raft made of balsa wood which is found at the southern end of the lake.

Somewhat resembling a very miniature baobab tree but with resplendant flowers, the desert rose (Adenium obesum) can be found on most islands. True to its name, this plant grows between the lava rocks and in almost impossible places.

Photo on page 53 : high- and low-water levels have greatly influenced Lake Baringo. The high-water line drops when the rains fail, as in 1961 and 1971, and rises with abundant rainfall as in 1978. The difference can clearly be seen on the rocks standing in the water, and may be anything up to 6 feet (2 metres).

Scientists warn that the lake, which has no inlet, will be quite dry in fifty years' time.

Aerial photograph of Lake Baringo and its surroundings. In the foreground one can clearly distinguish the bomas, huts for the natives surrounded by thorn bushes. Clearly visible also is the erosion caused by thousands of goats trotting daily to the lake to quench their thirst and which has stripped the grasslands and trek routes.

Following the example of the late David Roberts and Michael Skinner, I was not scared by the proximity of crocodiles and hippos, and searched for relief from the heat in the brown tepid water of Lake Baringo The fact that the reptiles are not dangerous is said to be because of the abundance of fish in this lake. So far, the water is fortunately free from bilharzia — a tropical parasitic worm which is to be found in nearly all stagnant waters in Africa. However, the rise in population around the lake, may alter this.

Formerly, Lake Baringo was surrounded by forests inhabited by elephants, leopards, giraffes and antelopes. The animals have vanished. Man with his cattle has taken over, hacking down the shady trees to make firewood or charcoal. Gradually the area around the delightful lake is becoming an arid desert.

Three tribes live around and near Lake Baringo. The Njemps or Il-Tiamus, Masai in origin and greatly resembling them, settled at Lake Baringo and successfully concentrated on agriculture. About 1880 they supplied food to Jozef Thomson and Count Teleki when they were exploring the district. Ever since then they have supplied passing caravans with food. Their cultural pattern, their *mayattas* (huts), their mode of life and their dances resemble the Masai. Until recently, it was the habit of the Eastern Suk (page 56) to weave the hair of their dead father into their own hair and form a kind of chignon. This was then covered with clay and the white of ostrich-eggs and finally painted blue. On festive occasions, all this was completed with an enormous ostrich-feather.

The Suk believe in one god. A god which they call the air *(terorut)* and his son, the rain *(ilat)*. They worship snakes and when one enters their hut, it must not be killed but be presented with a dish of milk. A Suk may have as many women as he can support.

The Pokot women (photo 57 above) dress in goats' skins. In their typical backpacks they transport milk or the precious water of Lake Baringo to their huts which may be some distance from the lake. For many of them, the daily task is to fetch the indispensable water while herding their goats. Their decorations of beads and brass rings are impressive. In 1963 I was fortunate in photographing a woman wearing a most artistic apron, which at that time was very fashionable. Yet, I have never seen it since. Folklore and the cultural pattern are also rapidly vanishing, as is the landscape, once so very beautiful, around Lake Baringo.

Goats, those all-devouring creatures, are devastating the vegetation. While they are, themselves, a source of food they cause terrible erosion and are a classic example of incorrect land use. They are destroying the unique natural paradise of Baringo.

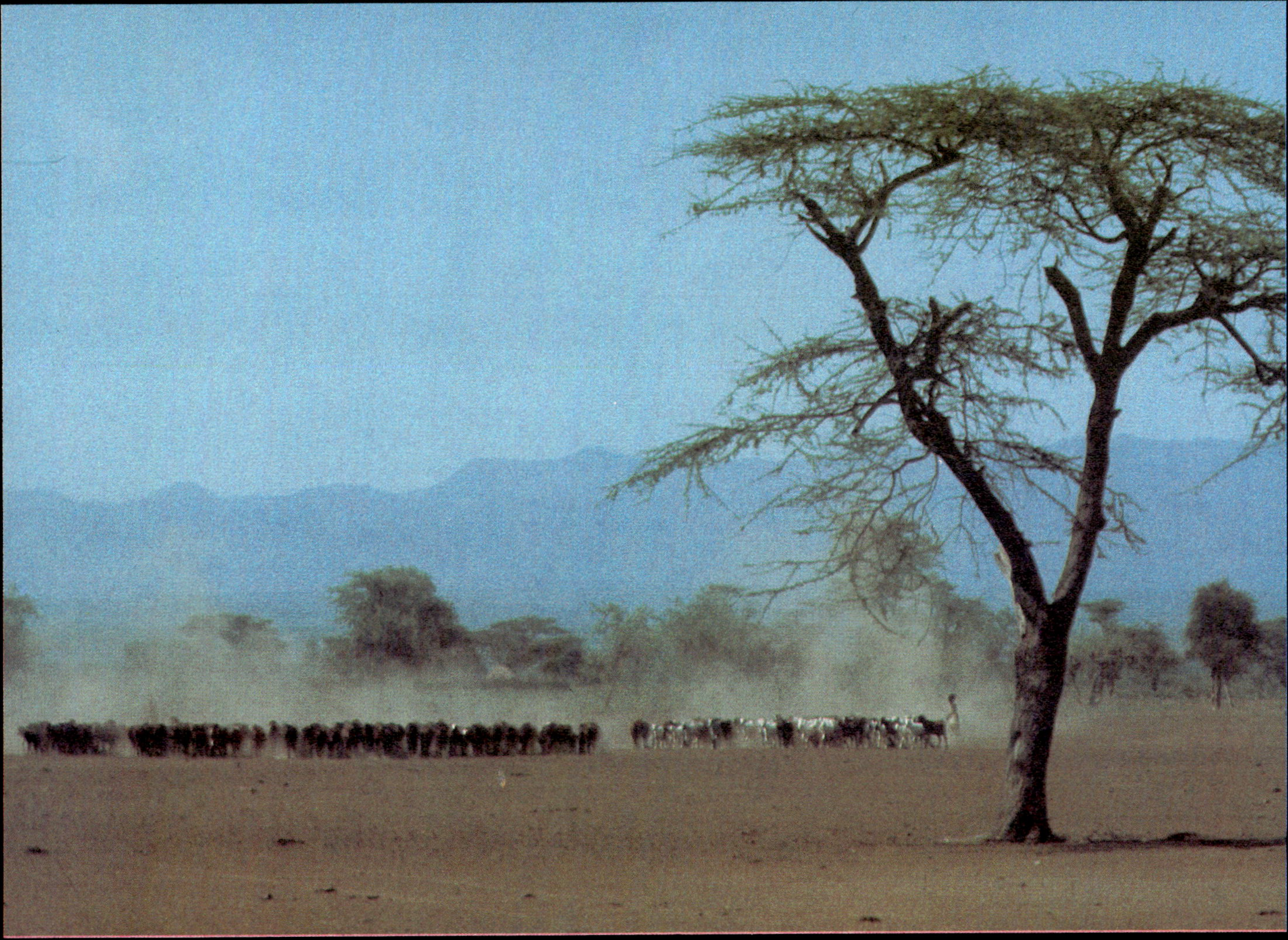

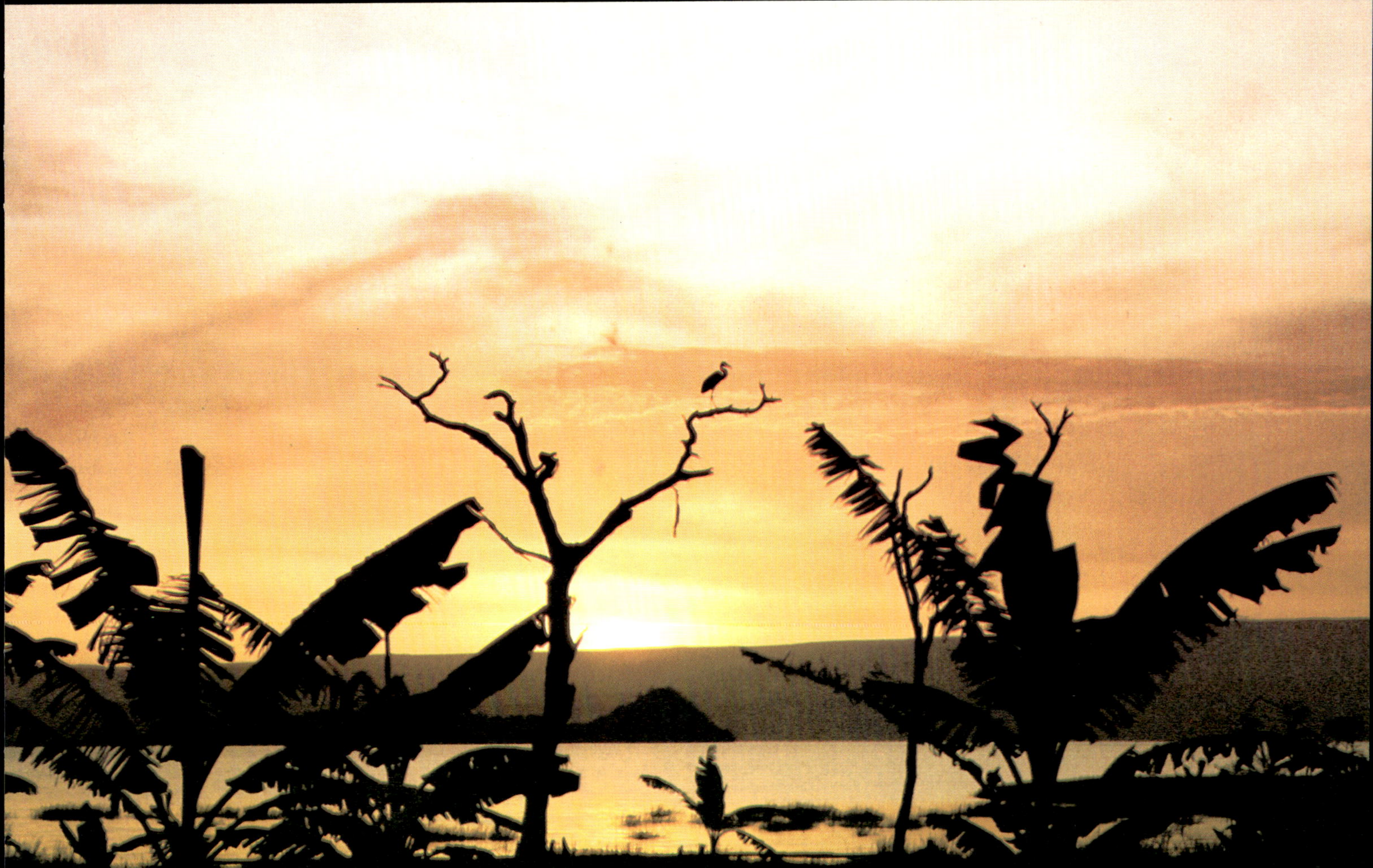

Crocodiles

Living fossils

Crocodiles are such pleasant fellows. One of my cameras knows all about that. It happened during a visit to a crocodile farm in Rhodesia, where a breeding establishment for these reptiles can be visited by tourists, and a solid catwalk passes over the breeding ponds.

An agreement with the Wild Life Department determines that crocodile eggs along the banks of the Zambezi River may be collected for incubation on condition that five per cent of the reptiles are returned to the Zambesi – whatever happens. The artificially hatched eggs are then placed in rearing ponds. These ponds keep the young of one up to six years old apart from each other. When they are six years old, the crocodiles have the impressive length of nearly 5 feet (1,50 metres) and are then slaughtered. Their skins serve to make women's handbags, men's belts and other fashion articles which are extremely popular.

Armed with only a stick, the crocodile expert stands amongst the reptiles and gives the tourists on the catwalk an interesting lecture. With the aid of living proof he provides the interested visitor with all the information any true nature lover would like to know about these hardly appealing reptiles.

Knowing my wish to film the reptiles at close range and in full movement, the obliging crocodile breeder invited me into the cage and ordered one of his African helpers to bring in a few buckets full of fish. Being, as always, interested in *verité* pictures, I asked the Rhodesian to have the fish thrown to a specific point, 6 feet (2 metres) in front of me in the pool. 'Yes, over there, just there.' At that spot, maybe a throng of them, the creatures would open their jaws. For the time being about one hundred six year olds were lying like a ball which could not be disentangled; immobile in the hot sun in the far left-hand corner of the enclosed space (55 yards/ 50 metres long), dreaming, no doubt, their reptilian dreams.

I was ready to shoot, resting on one knee, camera prepared. Through my viewfinder I could only see what was going to happen in a small circle 6 1/2 feet (2 metres) in front of me. To the right of my foot was my still camera, a faithful Leica, habitual, placed there so that if the film clip came to an end I could shoot some still photographs.

Much quicker than expected the reptiles raced, dived and spluttered in the

l would not have the courage even to dip my toe into the water near this 12 feet (4 metres) long colossus on the Tana River in Kenya.

The Njemp tribe around Lake Baringo, which we mentioned in the previous chapter, entice crocodiles to approach by making a sound resembling 'eem, eem, eem' just above the water level, pinching their nostrils to get a deeper tone. Believe me, it works. Why crocodiles, which hardly ever produce a sound, react in this way is a mystery to me !

Besides fish, which they gulp down whole, crocodiles greedily eat any living creature which does not appear too large or too heavy. They hide their prey under water between tree-trunks or in cracks in the rocks and leave it there to decompose – not because they are fond of rotting food, but because they have to wait until it is easier to digest. They can only tear pieces from their prey. Their teeth snap close and they can bite and chew, but cannot grind.

water in order to gobble as much food as possible in the shortest possible time. The picture in my viewfinder was promising. Wide-open muzzles with enough yellow-orange throats and serried rows of teeth to make one's hair stand on end.

I enjoyed it, until suddenly I heard a blood-curling yell from all the tourists on the catwalk above us. Looking away from my film camera, I quickly spotted an enormous crocodile close to my right leg. It had grabbed my camera and turning on its axis had already started on its way back to the pool. The Rhodesian standing to my left hit the monster with his stick over my shoulder, but too late … Whether the crocodile consumed my camera or dropped it in the pond, I cannot tell. The fact is that my very expensive, well-loved camera was irretrievably lost. An easy victim of a hungry crocodile !

When I asked whether my camera could ever be recovered, the Rhodesian promptly replied that the ponds would be cleaned within three months and if it had ended up in the stomach of the crocodile, well, the reptiles would be slaughtered in August and I would be informed.
That was the last I ever saw of my camera.
Crocodiles are such pleasant fellows !

RHODESIA, 1974

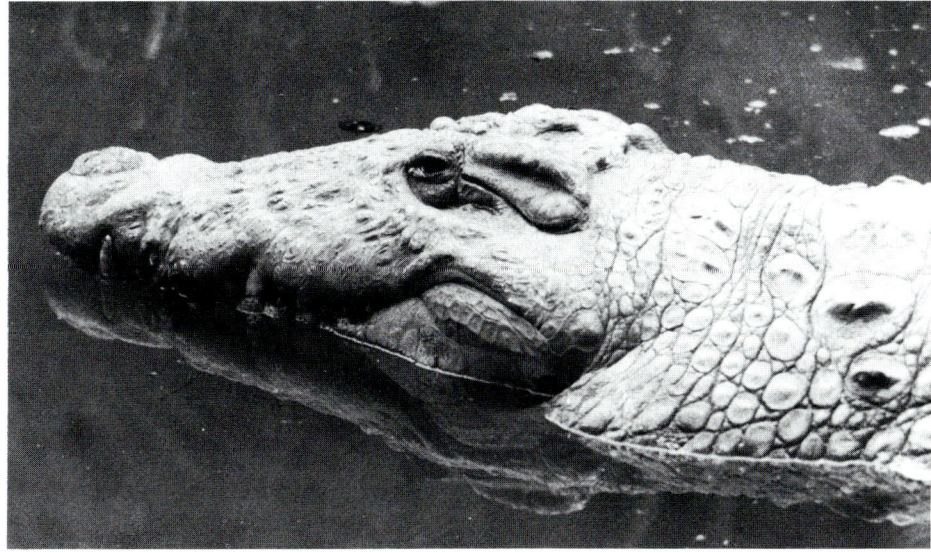

Lions

'The lion is an animal with no fear for anybody', said my teacher, when as a small boy I listened in rapture to everything remotely connected with wild animals. Although I have since acquired some doubts about Leo, *Leo rex*, King of the animals, I still approach them with the greatest respect.

Anybody who has ever encountered on foot an adult lion in the African jungle will share my feelings. A person who has seen a lion attacking and striking down a buffalo; who has stood beside a hunter when a lion with a speed of six seconds per 110 yards (100 metres) charges, will have nothing but respect and will not play little tricks with him !

Lions are excellent killers. It is their task in life, their ecological role. They keep wild life in check, clear up sick, weak and unhealthy animals – in short, they play a useful function in nature. Though more of a day-time beast of prey than any other of the feline species, they still prefer to hunt at night.

They are not fussy in the choice of their prey, but adjust to the circumstances, to the stock which is available. In the one place this may be buffaloes, in another zebras or gnus. A lion eats 9 to 13 pounds (4 to 6 kilogrammes) of meat a day, but can easily gorge 44 pounds (20 kilogrammes) all at once. Lions kill probably once a week, but with a prey of 660 pounds (300 kilogrammes) they can last for a while longer. They kill only when they are hungry. Besides the meat, they also devour the intestines filled with half digested grasses. Most probably this is the way they acquire the amount of vitamins that they need.

In times of drought or great food scarcity, lions manage to eat large

Early one morning, this young but already quite developed lion passed our encampment, which we had erected along the Uaso Nyiro River.

numbers of insect-beetles etc. In turn, they are greatly troubled by insects. There are numerous varieties of stable-flies in Africa. The tsetse-fly (*Glossina*), the horse-fly (*Tabanidae*) and the freakish flies (*Hippoboscidae*) cling to the lion's manes. Besides the great variety of stable-flies, the lions also attract numbers of ordinary fly-species, blue meat-flies and insects, owing to the smell of flesh which constantly surrounds them. With these pests all around him, it is not surprising that the lion is often extremely bad-tempered and will move from one place to another. In the Ngorongoro-crater in Tanzania the lions are sometimes pestered to such an extent by the *Stomoxys* flies that they either die or leave the place altogether. Also the Siafu ants, attracted by the smell of blood, are a plague to the lions. Ticks must not be forgotten, lions have them in series; they collect them in the grass or from the recently killed prey. As soon as a killed animal gets cold, the ticks search for another source of life. In this way the lions are the host to numerous guest workers and their lives are not all that easy ...

My first real encounter with a lion took place in the Serengeti-plain of Tanzania (at the time still Tanganika) in 1962. Gordon had parked the Land-Rover in the shade of a yellow-fever tree (*Acacia xanthophloea*) and was enjoying an inevitable cup of tea. As I had been in the car for many hours I decided to stretch my legs, so I climbed the enormous rock formation which was standing proudly in the extensive Serengeti plain and called locally by the South African name of kopjes or koppies. Enormous monolithic blocks lay spreading over the endless grassy plain. By climbing the least steep sides one can reach the top of these 100 feet (30 metres) high rocks. Thinking of that enormous space, I thought I would be able to take some interesting shots from the top. Puffing in the African afternoon heat I had nearly reached the top when, suddenly over the edge of the rocks, I first spied the ears and then the eyes of a most surprised lioness.

Mating lions in Virunga National Park, Zaire. During mating the female withdraws with her selected partner into the bushes, far away from the group. Their love-play continues for a few days and is repeated every twelve minutes or so.

With not a moment's hesitation I raced as quickly down the slope as possible, with little doubt breaking world records in my flight. Utterly exhausted and trembling from head to foot I fell down beside Gordon

Harvey and spluttered that I had been eye-to-eye with a lion. To cap it all, I got a most severe reprimand from my Scottish friend. 'Never run away from a lion', he said severely. 'You should know that cat-like animals are inclined to jump after their prey.' At my timid request as to what I should have done, I received the brisk reply : 'Ignore her.' Probably, the poor lioness had been equally frightened and had run down the other side of the koppie with equal speed.

Only when surrounded by cubs (and a lioness just like a leopardess often retires into these rock formations to give birth to their young) would she be dangerous. In order to protect her cubs, the lioness would attack.

'All right,' I told Gordon, 'and if she had attacked, what should I have done then ?'

'Next question', said Harvey.

Older males, who have had enough of family life or are tired of the vigorous romping of the young, sometimes retire in groups or couples to live in peace.

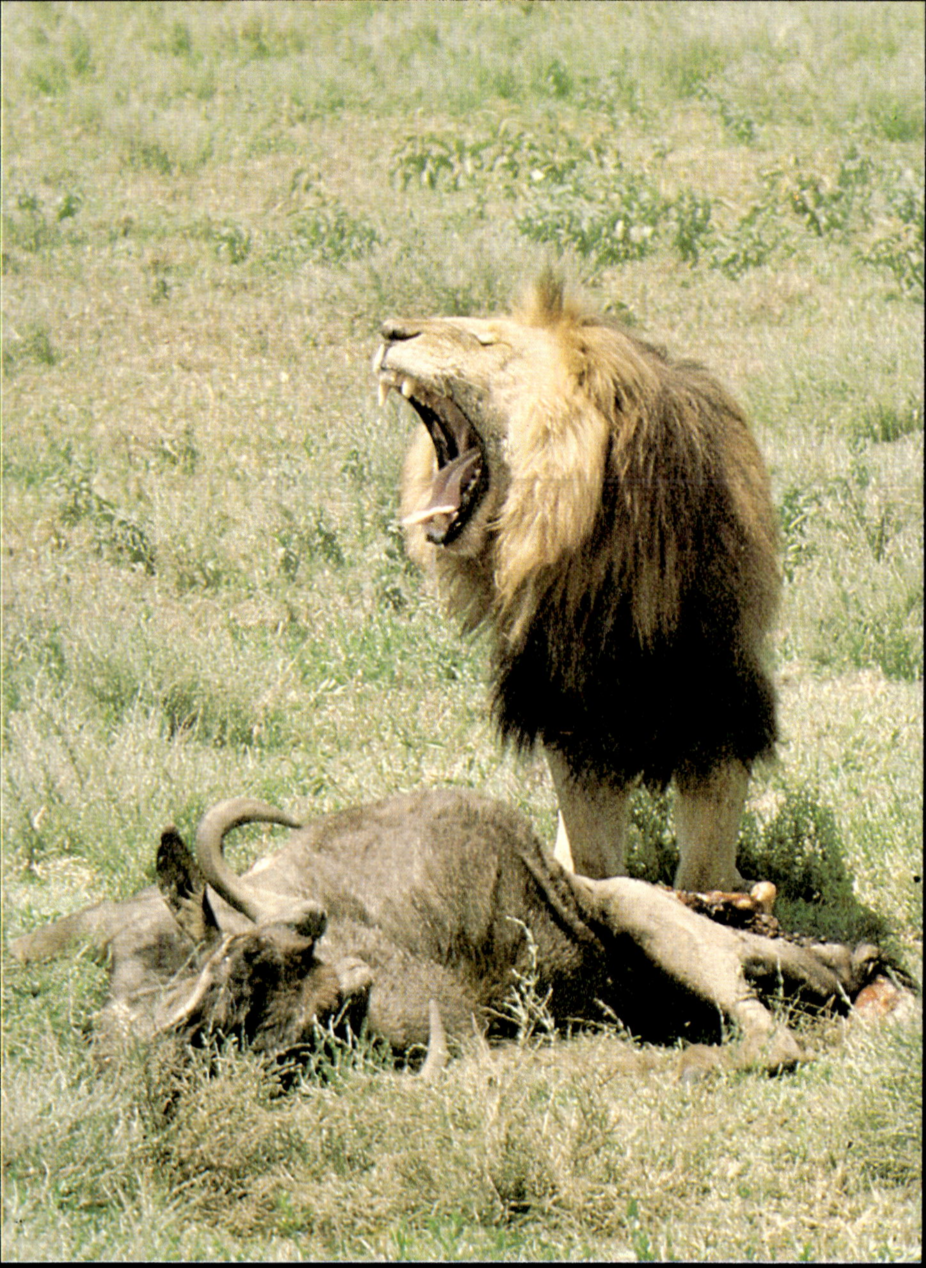

The undisputed ruler of the African savannahs with his prey, a gnu-antelope.

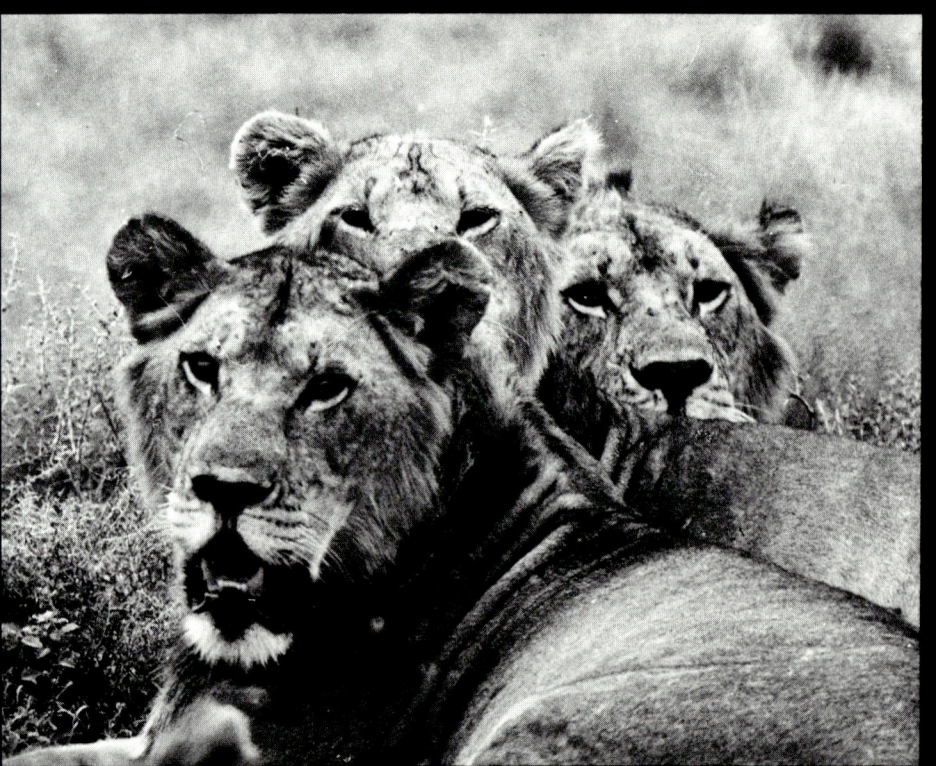

Usually the lionesses organise the hunt. Three or four together stalk a prey or course it towards each other. This is often more rewarding than approaching a herd alone.

Simba

Only rarely do lions attack people – they prefer a nice juicy zebra of some 660 pounds (300 kilogrammes). Only the old and toothless lions – rejected from the pride and too weak to catch a quick antelope – may assault man. Then, hidden near a river, it is quite simple to attack a woman or a child collecting water.

It often surprises me that the great and mighty beast of prey, which the lion is, has such a great respect for human life. After all, that weak, hesitating, timid creature on two legs, who is petrified by fear at the sign of danger, is no match. Is there an easier prey than man ? Or is human flesh so bitter ? Does it not taste good ? Or is the fear for our weapons, together with our smells, deep in their nostrils ?

Yet in the last century, during the construction of the railway line Mombasa-Nairobi, in the present Tsavo region, dozens of Indians were killed. I was thinking of that, when camping once again with Gordon in the east Tsavo, the region above the Galana River. We had opened up our tents in the shade of a row of palm trees.

I had just finished my film – Tiva-death and life of a river. The dried-up river was dying in the sweltering sun. The heat was unbearable. The hot wind, blowing from the Indian Ocean, carried the nauseating smell of the carcasses of elephants, rhinos and buffaloes killed by the drought. It was our last evening. In the morning we would leave the Tiva and Tsavo. Meru was waiting for us to start a new stage.

I agreed with Gordon that we should break camp as much as possible the evening before, even to pulling down the tents, leaving only the camp-beds in the loose sand – above us some palm trees and an endless starry sky with the Southern Cross as a night lantern. Gordon's two African helpers, Daghoro and Joseph, a Tanzanian and a Kikuyu would sleep in a pocket-size tent. Their superstition, the fear of the evil spirit of the night, required them to do that.

It is one of the glorious experiences in a man's life to lie on a camp-bed in the middle of the African wilderness, hundreds of miles from the nearest point of civilisation. Above spreads the splendid starry sky, shimmering in all its glory, with, now and then, a falling star. All around crackle the sounds of the night, the millions of cicadas, crickets, locusts, tree fogs, nightjars, bats and then suddenly above, in the highly branched wide palm-fingers, the bush-baby or galago (sometimes called komba, a type of half-monkey and night animal).

This was probably the thick-tailed galago (*Galago crassicaudatos*). His voice is clearer and his cry louder than that of the dwarf galago which was so well-known to me from the Aberdare Mountains or the forest around Elgon. Like all galagos, he is very noisy during the night and produces the sounds of a child. I heard him in the crackling dry leaves jumping to and fro catching insects in flight. It is unbelievable how, in the nearly complete darkness, galagos catch prey on the wing during their leaps – prey as small as an insect.

Their enormous eyes – very large, bullet-round organs with excellent vision even with the slightest ray of light – play an important part. I moved my tape recorder, which I always keep handy, from below my camp-bed. I listened. Some cries of the night animals are far from melodious, they sound like a creaking shed door. It is easy to understand that natives think these sounds come from evil spirits. Joseph and Daghoro would be stiff with fright.

Suddenly the sounds stopped. Not only of the galagos, the cicadas also were silent. Even the wind had dropped, or was this purely my imagination ? It was deadly quiet – too quiet. Relieved of all disturbing sounds I drowsed. A sudden unearthly roar tore the peace apart. Never had I heard that noise before. My heart stopped beating. The roaring, to the left at a distance of less than 30 feet (10 metres), was answered by a roar from the right – further away, perhaps 90 feet (30 - 50 metres) ? My tape recorder was still going – I suddenly remembered ! I was on a camp-bed without the least protection !

The roaring continued, dangerously close now – but I saw nothing. In vain I tried to see the yellow lights in the eyes of the beast – to my right were the bushes. Behind them or in the middle of them was the serenading lion. And here were we, Gordon and I, under the starry sky; without the least protection. Even the camp-fire was out. What chance did we have ? The car was some distance away. Then another roar. I was frightened stiff. The roar of a lion can be heard over a distance of 3 miles (5 kilometres) – imagine how it sounds at 32 feet (10 metres) !

Gordon says that the roaring of the 'king of the beasts', expressed in English, means 'Who is the master of this land ? I am ! I am ! I am !'

Utter fear got hold of me. This, I realised, was the district of 'The Man-eaters of Tsavo'. The man-eaters which stopped the construction of the railway line from Mombassa to Lake Victoria by killing more than thirty of the Indian navvies brought by the English from their country to build the permanent way.

Suddenly, the roaring stopped. The silence was awful. I dared not move. The cicadas then continued their monotous sound, but the galagos remained silent. 'Are you asleep, Gordon ?' I whispered. 'How would that be possible ?' was the soft reply. 'I have the most perfect lion concert you could wish for on my tape recorder,' said I.'For God's sake, don't play it back', pleaded Gordon. 'If they hear it, they will be back in a minute. Probably an engaged couple.'

I did not sleep much that night and I felt relieved when dawn broke and the pigeons and the starlings started their morning song.

Daghoro and Joseph, grey with fright, emerged from their tent only when Gordon started rattling the coffee-pot and kettles. With eyes wide open they told us that their small tent – some 55 yards (50 metres) from our sleeping place – had been visited by the lioness. Tightly closed in the front and back, they showed the damp spot where the lioness had made water against the tentcloth. The smell had kept them awake throughout the night and would continue to keep us company for our entire return journey !

TIVA, TSAVO EAST KENYA 1975

Our encampment underneath the doum palms (Hyphaene coriacea) *at the dry Tiva River.*

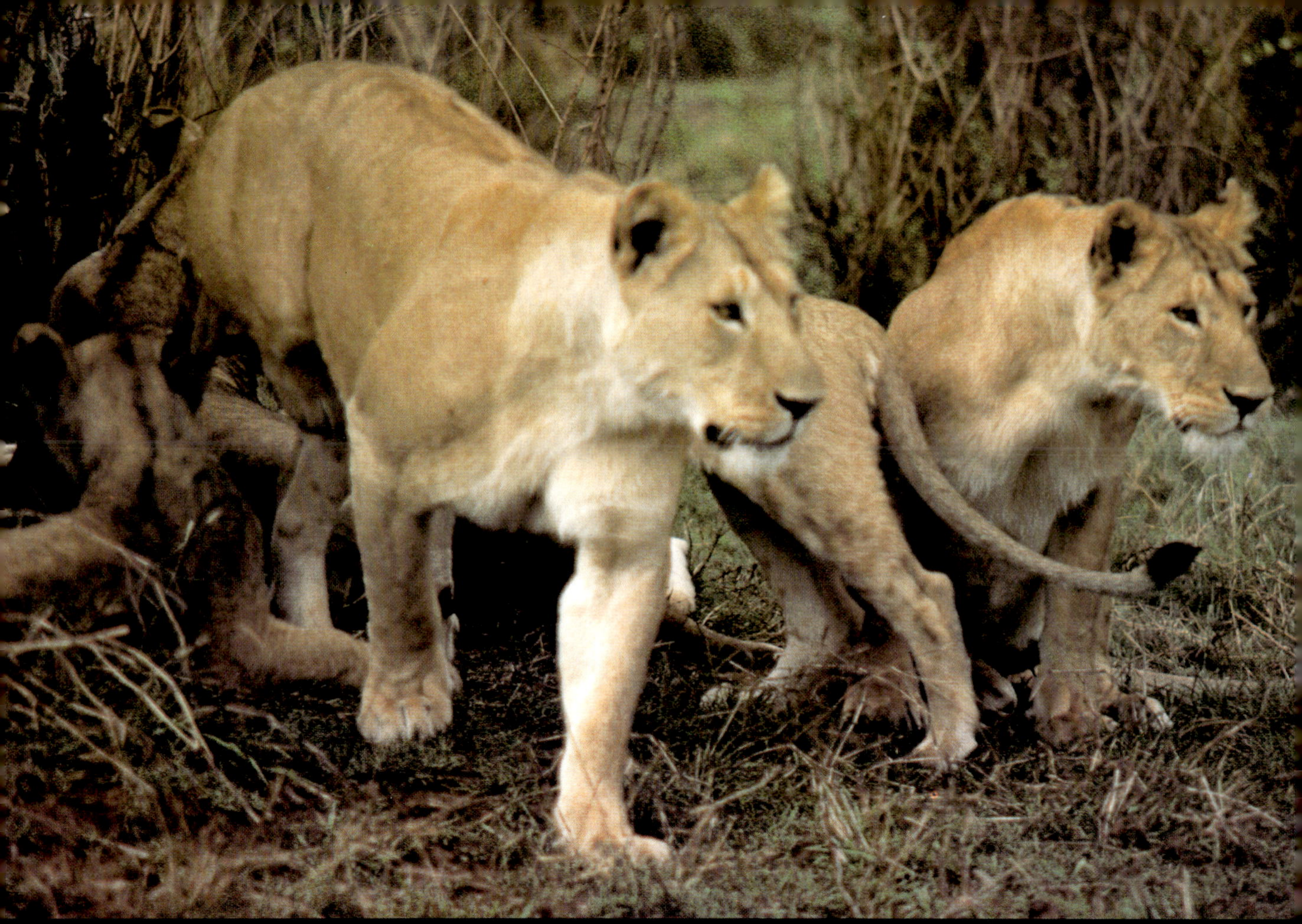

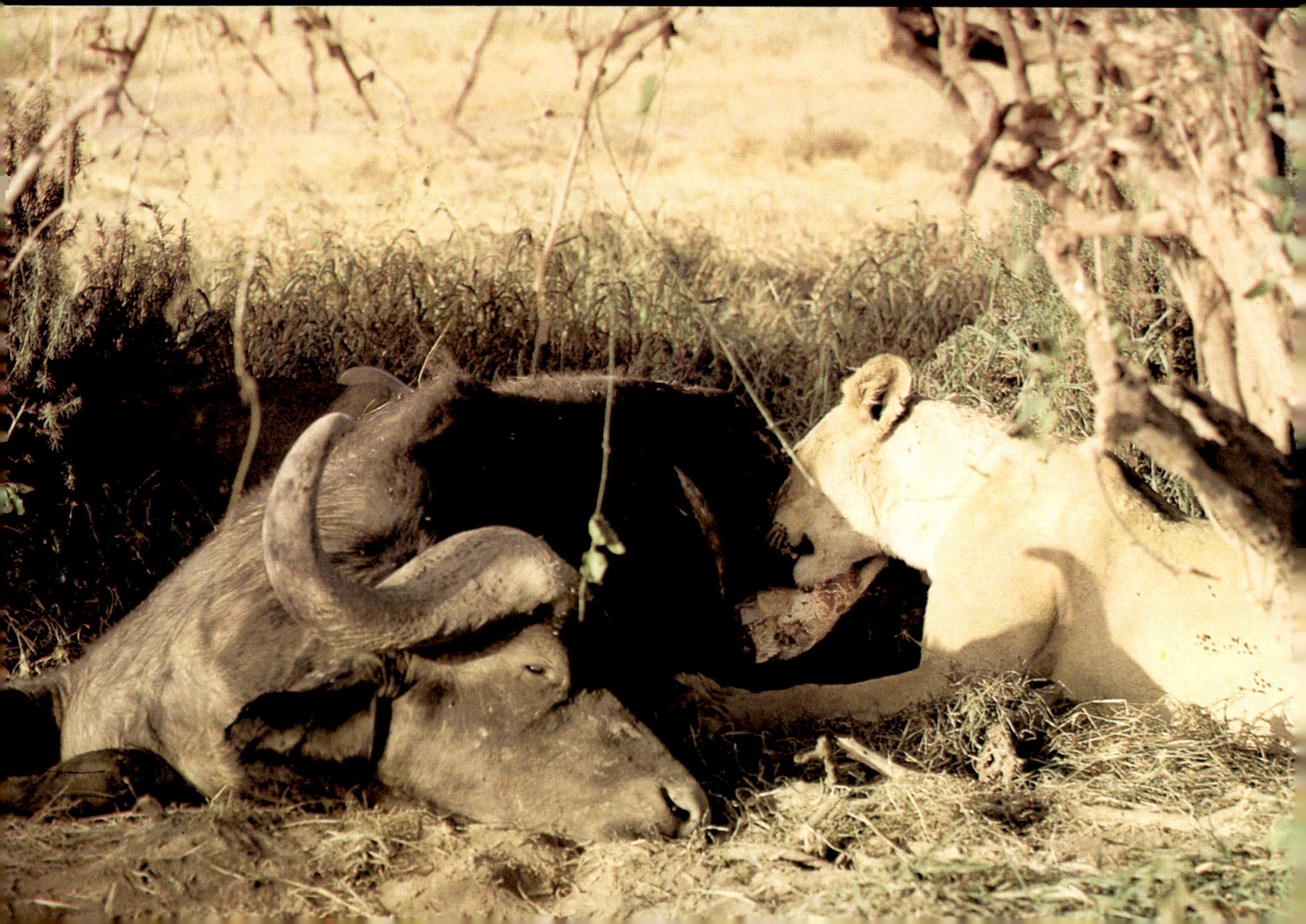

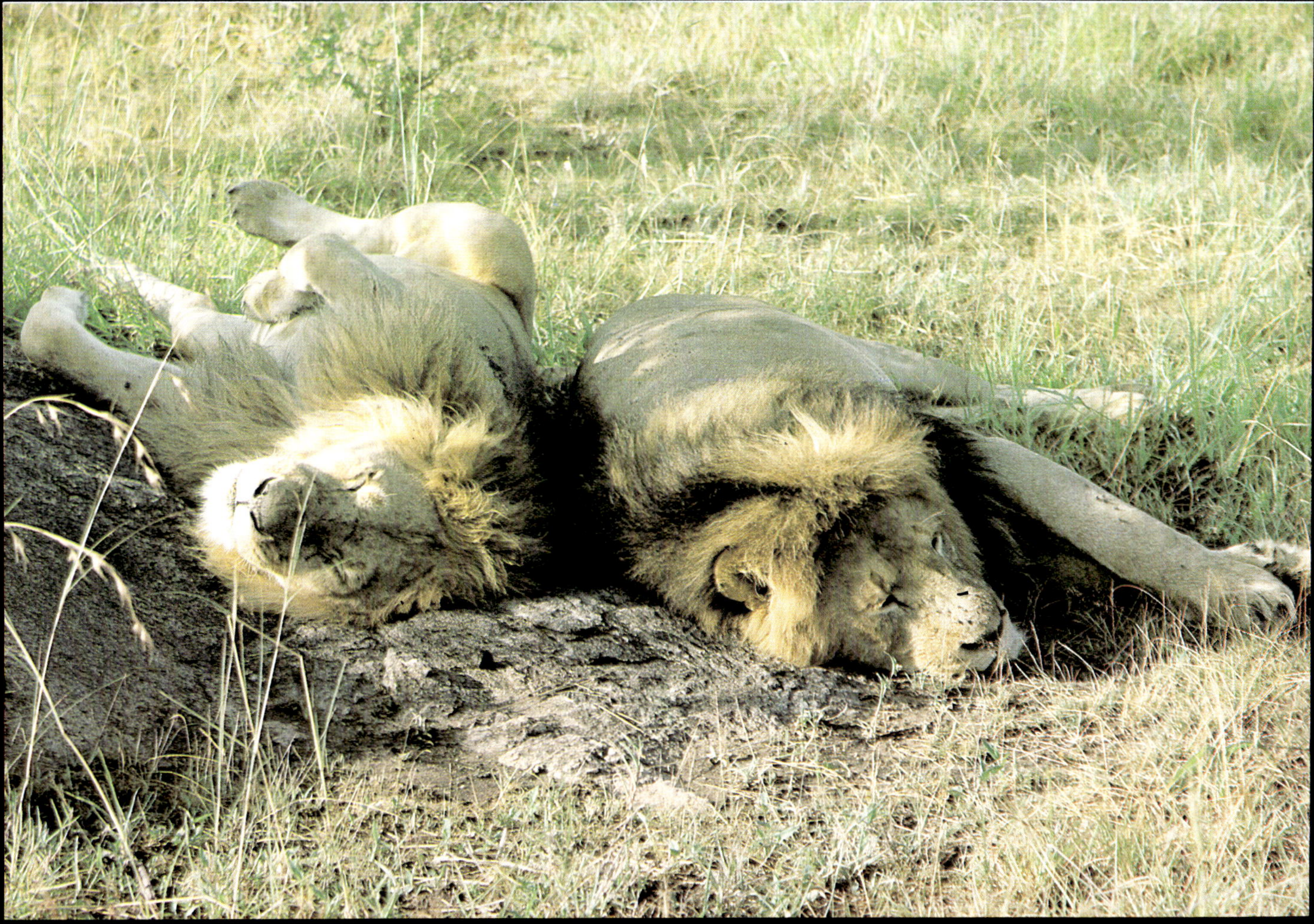

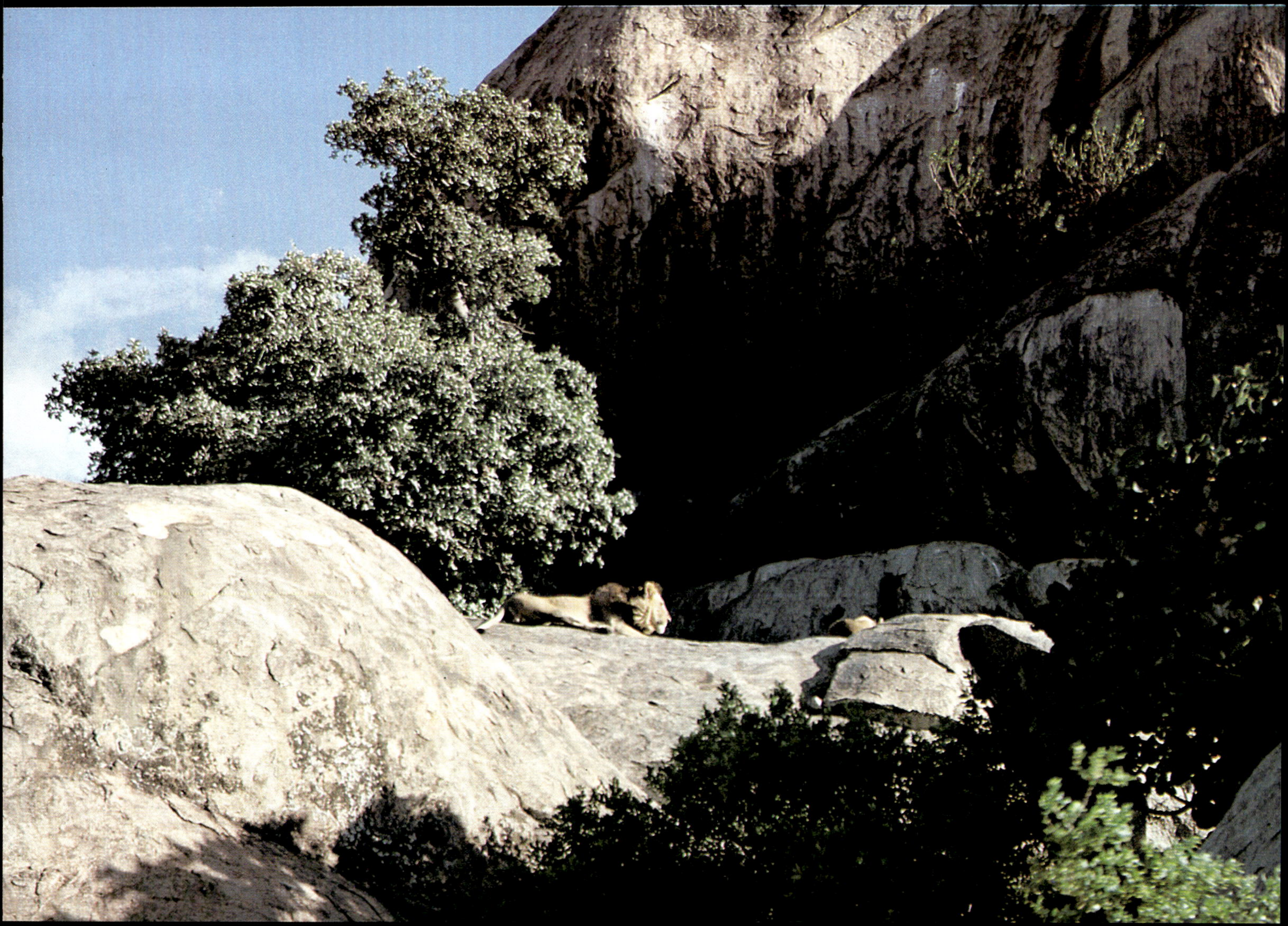

Serengeti

The Serengeti Plain has become well known through Dr Bernard Grzimek and his book; *Serengeti Shall not Die*. I shall never forget the overpowering impression the plain made on me when I saw it for the first time, nearly twenty years ago. I was accompanied only by my African driver and had just left another wonder of nature, the Ngorongoro crater. The Serengeti National Park covers some 8,000 square miles (13,000 square kilometres) stretching from the Ngorongoro crater wall in the south to the border with Kenya in the north and the banks of Lake Victoria in the west. The name Serengeti comes from the Masai *Siringet*, which roughly means 'extensive plain'.

Despite its tremendous size and the strenuous efforts made by conservationists, attempts to make an ecological unit of this jewel of national parks have not succeeded. Animals do not recognise boundaries and they wander freely in and out of the park and across the borders of countries, according the season and obeying innate behaviour patterns. At certain times of the year , these areas appear to be totally deserted, but during the rainy season, between November and May, the grass steppes become feeding grounds for some 350,000 wildebeests or gnus, 180,000 Burchell zebras, more than half a million Thomson and Grant gazelles, ostriches, elands, hartebeests and topi antelopes, and large and small beasts of prey following the herds.

The dominant tree in Serengeti is the umbrella tree *(Acacia tortillis)*. It provides the lions with shade, and the giraffes with a source of food. From the kopjes or koppies, a word taken by the British from the South African word which refers to the enormous granite rocky mounds dispersed across the endless plain, one has superb views of the vast expanse. These mounds have their own flora and fauna : for example, Johnston's hyrax or coneys *(Procavia johnstoni)* sometimes called 'dassie' in South Africa, are typical inhabitants of these hills. It is remarkable that this animal resembling a rabbit is closely related to the elephant – at least, according to scientists and based on its anatomical structure (centre photo). In between and deep inside the fissures of the mounds there are nkongi or wild sisal *(Sansevieria robusta)*, that are used by the natives for making strings for their bows. Elephants like to chew it and the British call it 'bowling hemp' (see bottom photo on page 72).

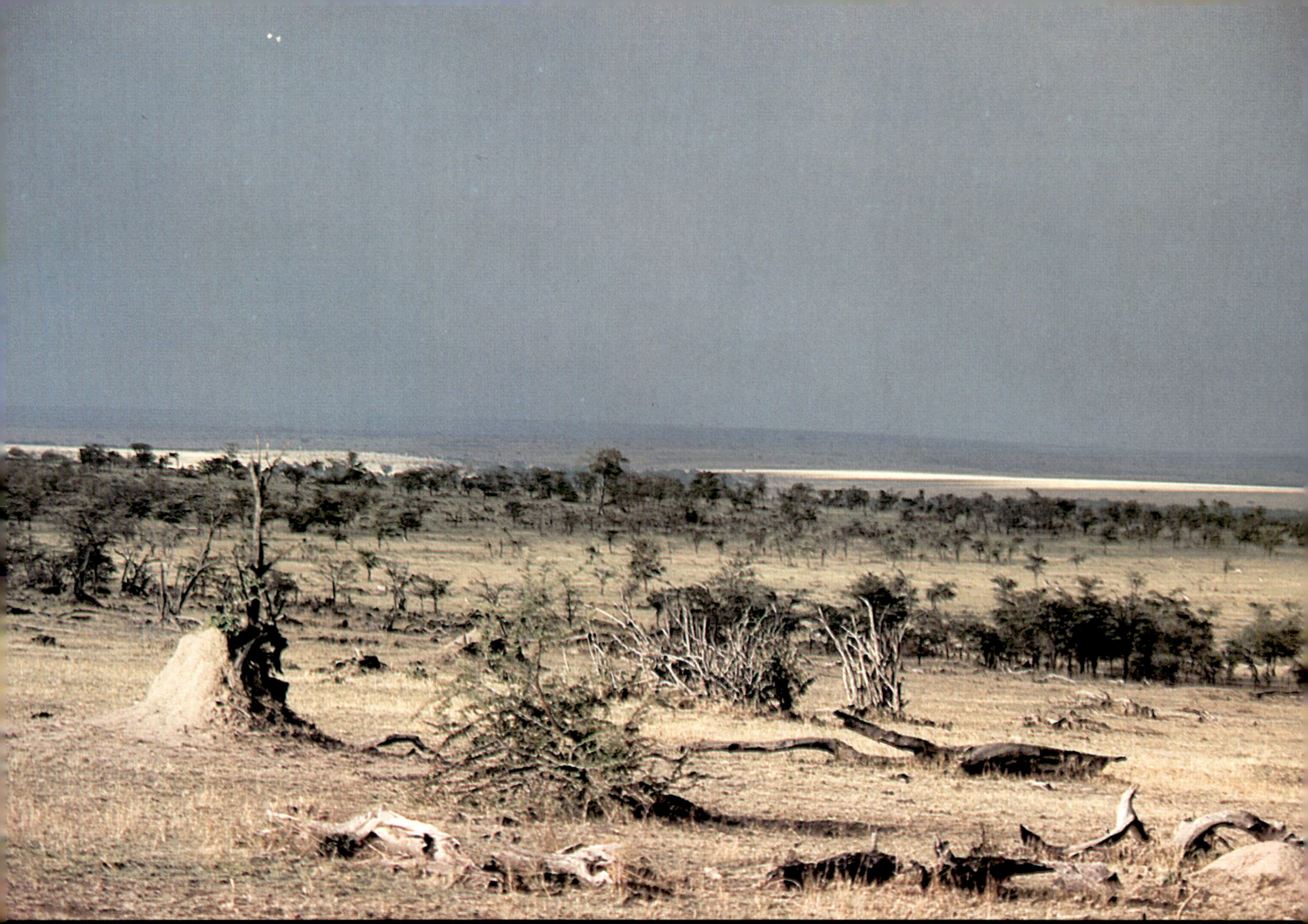

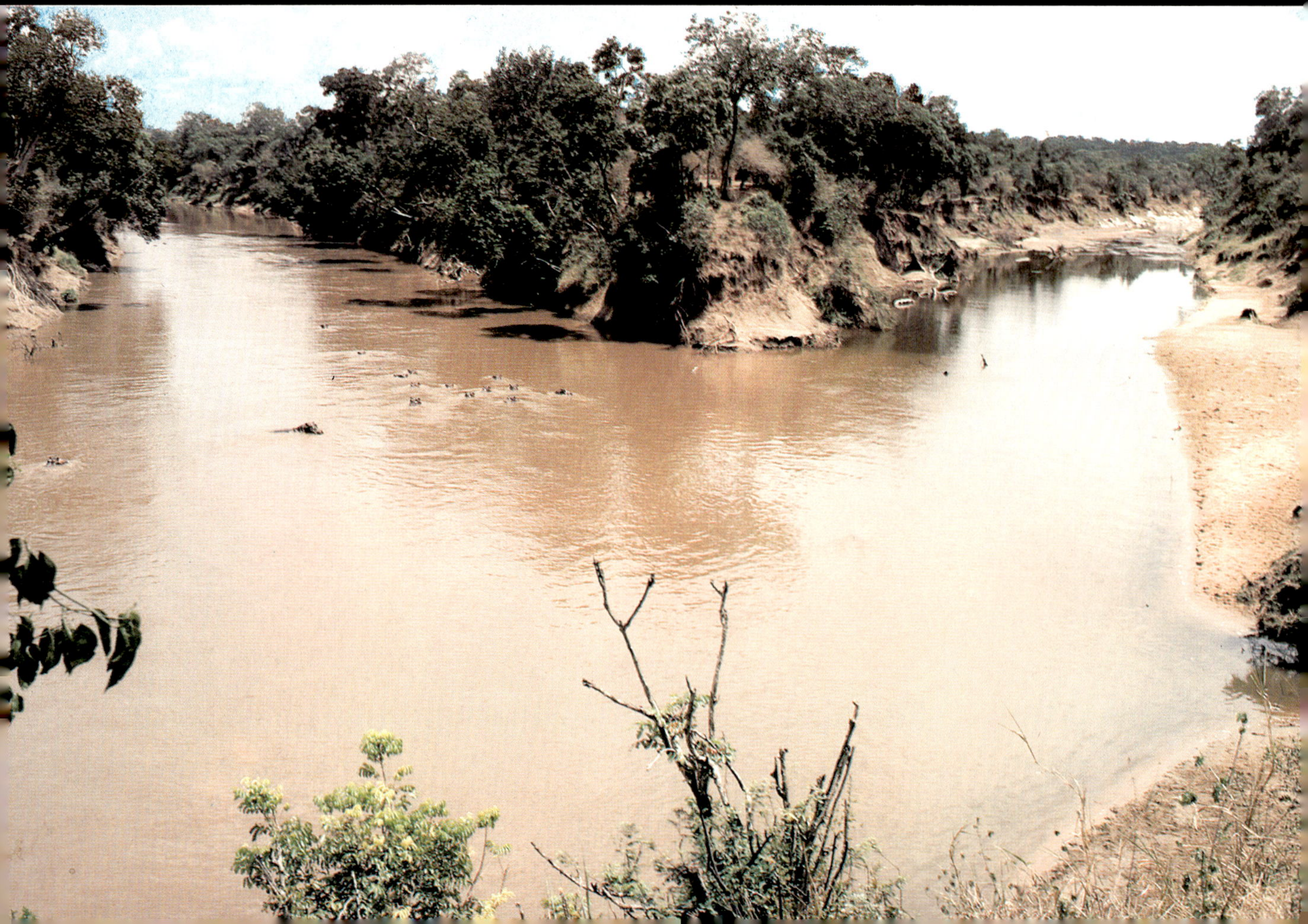

Talking about zebras

The Masai-Mara plain before a tropical thunderstorm. The eastern sector of this wildlife reservation on the borders of Tanzania is considered to be the animal paradise of Kenya.

The little tuft of grass which was supposed to protect and hide me was flattened by the hot wind. I was sitting behind a sand hill, squatting down, making myself as small as possible. Figuratively and literally I looked grey. The yellow-grey dust through which nothing could be seen enveloped me and almost prevented me from breathing. It was stuck to my sweating skin and gave me an excellent camouflage. It would not be long before I would look like a sand heap myself. I could not see anything any more, I only heard the sound of the roaring wind and hoof-beats vanishing in the distance, far away, belonging to zebras. I felt low. How did I get here ? What was I doing here on this enormous sand plateau, hundreds and hundreds of miles away from civilisation – on my haunches, wearing nothing but shorts and sandals, bent forward over a heavy cine-camera, which I was trying to protect against the penetrating dust; with a blinding, roaring yellow-grey sandstorm all around me.

Camping in the Nguruman massif at the border between Kenya and Tanzania I had driven into the lowlands with my African helper, Peter Kanyari. Up high, where our tents had been pitched, we could enjoy one of the most beautiful views in East Africa : Suswa, the Ngong mountains, Olorgesaile, Lake Magadi, Ol Doinyo Orok, Mosonik and Ol Doinyo

Bottom left : The joining of the Mara (left) and the Talek Rivers in the Masai-Mara region.

Sapuk. In front of us was the Great Rift. But there were no animals there, except for the turacos and a lonely leopard who during the night made his presence known by his 'sawing'. From our vantage point and with the aid of my field-glasses I had spotted quite a number of hoofed animals in the lower plain.

So we descended the mountain path – if you could call this track with enormous boulders and pot-holes by that gentle name – and drove through the burning, dry, white – yellow sand desert, sparsely dotted with slanting umbrella trees and a few sand hills. All this against a mighty mountain range, serene, grey-blue. We met zebras, oryx and giraffes. Considering the surroundings and the smooth site, I thought the place well suited for an experiment. My companion Kanyari had replaced Gordon Harvey on this safari (as Gordon had again gone to a Nairobi hospital for another operation) and together we entered the sandy desert on this fairly quiet, grey day. With the sun out it would become one of those hot, burning days, so normal here in this far-away corner of south Kenya in January. The heat was oppressive and heavy, which was why I wore only shorts. I discussed my plan with Peter.

If a herd of zebras came into sight, he would stop at a bush or slope. I would slide out of the car and hide behind it. Peter would then move off, or at least give the zebras the impression that he was doing so. In fact, he would make a wide circle around them in order to drive them in my direction. At the very last moment, and only then, would I leave my cover and film the zebra herd running towards me. I was well aware that, as soon as they became conscious of a human being, they would change their direction and vanish, either to the right or left, in an enormous cloud of dust. That was precisely my intention.

I had put my camera at slow-motion. Delayed shots would, in my

An anomaly in the zebra world. A wholly black zebra with white stripes. A topsy-turvy world – normally zebras are white with black stripes. Photograph taken in the Amboseli Reserve in 1966.

During my camel safari in February 1970 my horse was devoured by lions, hence my acquaintance with zebrules (a cross between a zebra and a donkey) which accompanied us as pack-animals.

Grevy's zebra (Equus grevyi), certainly the most beautiful of all zebra species. According to the animal trapper Don Hunt, their numbers in the wild have fallen to below 4,000.

opinion, create a fantastic sequence of these decorative animals, the dust clouds and the beautiful movement. And there I sat, bent double behind my little hill. I heard the car vanish into the distance and glanced carefully over the slope and the meagre grass. Far away I saw through my field-glasses about thirty steppezebras. There were some very young ones amongst them, which increased the charm.

Careful not to reveal myself – zebras have excellent eyesight – I squatted even lower behind my mound. To make sure of the direction of the wind, I put my finger in my mouth and raised it above my head. But there was no breeze, not a zephyr.

Suddenly I noticed how quiet it was and how burning hot. The sky was no longer blue. It looked lead-grey and, to my right, turning to ink black. The endless sulphur-coloured plain contrasted sharply against the dark sky. My artistic heart swelled. In my mind I clearly saw the picture. The leaden sky – darkly contrasting with the grey-yellow plain and on it, as a keyboard, the black and white stripes of the storming zebras. A picture to fall on ones knees for, which, in fact I was doing. In the distance I heard the zebras whinney … for the last time.

The heat had become unbearable, a heat which was intensified by the sudden arrival of a hot scorching wind – a storm wind which quickly became a sandstorm; and I was in the middle of it.

Standing upright I tried to locate our vehicle – no vehicle anywhere; no zebras; only a thick yellow fog, a hot wind and the grey dust clinging to my sweating skin. Bending forward, I crouched over my camera trying to protect the precious gear with my body. All sorts of thoughts raced through my mind. How could Peter ever find me again ? His own tyre tracks had vanished long ago. What would happen to me if he could not find the place where he had dumped me ? To leave the spot would be suicidal. The sandstorm had been raging fiercely for more than an hour. It looked as if night had fallen. I could see no further than a couple of yards. When at last the storm subsided, I looked like a sandman.

Another half hour passed before I heard the most welcome honking horn of our vehicle – it was music to my ears. Madly I stood and waved on top of my sand-heap until Peter saw me.

When we started on our way back to the camp, I saw in the retracting greyness, to the left of the car, a naked tree. At the foot, still vigorously holding on with his front legs to the trunk, sat a male baboon. He was thickly covered in grey dust. Somewhat startled by the sudden appearance of the dusty steel vehicle, the *nyani* threw us a very sad glance. The fright was still deeply imprinted on his baboon face, he had an expression of 'Whatever next ?' and, looking at myself, I could understand his feelings : we had shared the same ghastly experience …

NGURUMAN, KENYA 1973

Burchell's zebras on the Serengeti Plain

Grevy's zebra with young.

Stripes
in nature

In northern Uganda I found another oddity – a complete herd of maneless zebras. Even Gordon did not know what to say about it. On the zebra's back there was the inevitable Piapiac (Ptilostosmos afer), a raven-like bird, which in that part of Africa uses large animals as a look-out for insects disturbed by grazing animals.

There are several kinds of zebras. The most southern variety – the Cape quagga (the name was given by the Boers, after the sound which is so typical of zebras : 'kwaga, kwaha, kwahawa' !) – was killed off in the last century by the South African Boers. The last one died on 12th August 1883 in the zoo in Amsterdam.

The most common is the Steppe zebra (there is some contradiction about their true Latin name, some say *Equus quagga*, others *Equus burchelli*, but both are practically extinct, Steppe zebra seems to be the best name). On the Serengeti plain in Tanzania there are still over a million left. There are some sub-species, such as the boemi, selous, Chapmans, and damaras. There are two other sub-varieties of mountain zebra, the rare Hartmann and the Cape mountain zebra. The further south one goes, the broader and fewer the striped markings on the zebra's coat become, contrary to up north, where the finely striped Grevy zebra lives.

The Grevy is very special not only for its finer stripes, but also for its general appearance. It is more like a donkey than the Steppe zebra, who resembles a small horse. There has been bad news recently about their numbers. During my safaris along the northern border of Kenya nearly twenty years ago, I filmed hundreds of these magnificent animals. According to a count made by Ian Grimwood, their numbers have dropped from 15,000 to just over one thousand ! The wars in Ethiopia, Somalia, and the Shifta in Kenya had all taken their toll ! The first things that troops, both regulars and mercenaries, shoot to eat are large animals : *nyama mkubwa*.

The largest and most attractive species of zebra was discovered in 1882. Only in this century, in 1905, the Emperor of Abyssinia (now Ethiopia) gave a live specimen to the third President of the French Republic, whose name was Jules Grevy, hence the attractive name given by the experts to this race. Now, within a century of their discovery, man is well on the way to exterminating them !

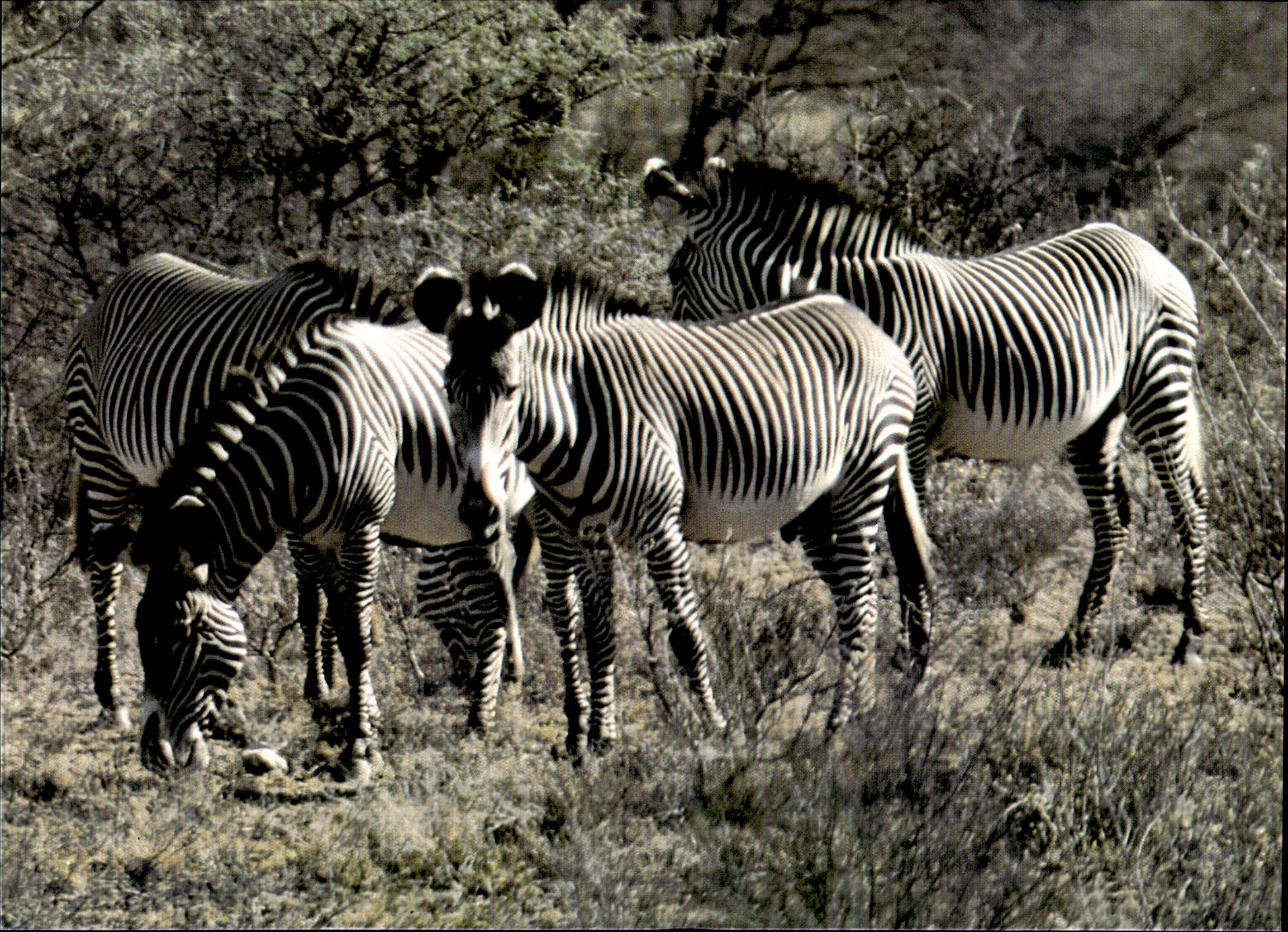

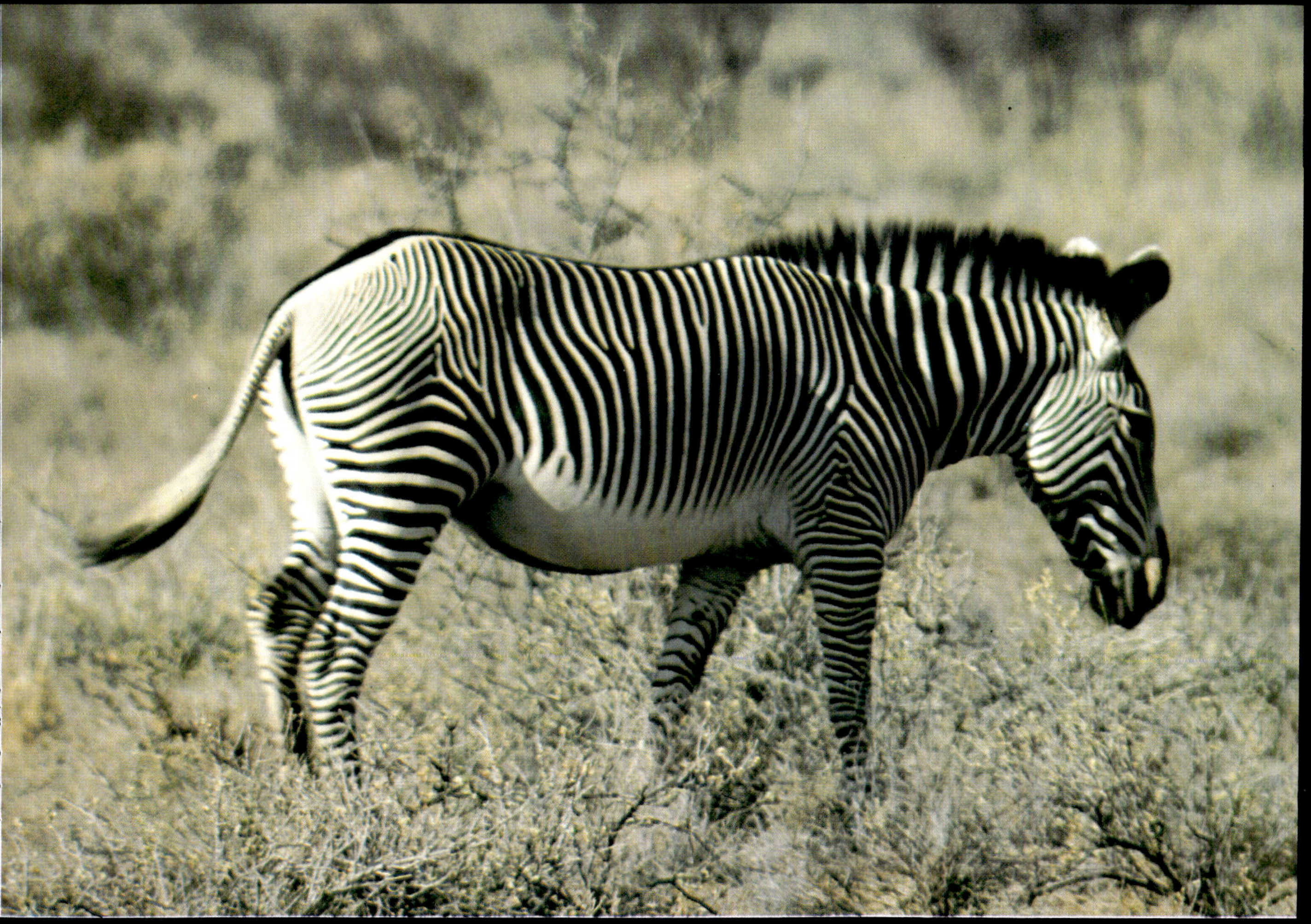

The three giraffe species of East Africa. Top left : the most common is the Masai giraffe (Giraffa camelopardis tippelskirchi). Top right and below left : the reticulated giraffe (Giraffa camelopardis reticulata).

Bottom right : Rothschild's or Uganda giraffes (Giraffa rothschildi) in the Kidepo region in north Uganda at the border with the Sudan. There are only some 150 of these remaining in Kenya and the fight is on for their survival.

Giraffes

Gordon Harvey often teased me about my weak spot for giraffes. The Scots are very thrifty and keep a close eye on their pennies, and it was always with a tone of amazement that Gordon said : 'but this is at least the thousandth giraffe you have photographed !' Indeed, I am in love with giraffes. Their calm sedateness, their dignified gait, their large eyes – the most beautiful eyes in the animal kingdom – fringed by long eyelashes, their variety of colour and design, for there are not two giraffes with the same markings. The Somali giraffe *(Giraffa reticulata)*, the Masai or East African giraffe *(Giraffa camelopardus tippelskirchi)* and the Uganda or Rothschild giraffe *(Giraffa camelopardalis rothschildi)* are three of the seven species now left in Africa, and the tallest of all mammals. Some have two, others five skin-covered horns. Their eyes are not only beautiful, but they are exceptionally sharp, and with them they look over the heads of all other animals. They are almost entirely mute, and very gentle – these aristocrats of the animal world.

Cheetahs

The world's swiftest animal

The fastest animal on earth was chasing the frightened Thompson gazelles. The mother antelope, with a very young baby beside her, had not observed the hunting cheetah which was stalking them in the high grass. When the predator suddenly shot towards her, she tried to escape with some sidewards leaps, but the speed of the cheetah was formidable. With one blow, which broke her neck, the young gazelle was instantly killed. With the small antelope hanging from her muzzle like a limp rag, the cheetah returned triumphantly to her own young, three almost grown animals who were now coming forward to meet their mother. While the young cheetahs were devouring the prey, mother cheetah watched over them, looking into the distance, probably worried that hyenas, jackals or lions would capture the kill. Mother cheetah will never touch the prey herself until her young have fed.

At some distance mother gazelle looked sadly on. The cruel law of the jungle had prevailed once more, her young had been taken in order to feed the young of others.

I had been able to film the entire drama, but in doing so had caused us to be some hours late. We had followed the hunting cheetah for quite a distance and were now far beyond the corridor which we normally followed when tracking through the Serengeti.

Night approached and enormous raindrops suddenly fell on our windscreen. The parched bushes needed some freshening, there had not been any rain for four months. But rain in Africa is no summer storm. The downpour just would not stop. The ditches through which we travelled had become streams. To crown it all, that part of the world is, to use the

Left. While three young ones are devouring a gazelle, the mother cheetah, who has killed it for them, carefully keeps guard. All too often the prey is stolen by lions or hyenas.

Hunting cheetahs on reconnaissance in the Serengeti. They never attack zebras, who are too large for them. For preference they hunt the Thompson's or Grant's gazelles, hares, guinea-fowl and smaller animals.

Unlike other spotted cats of prey, the hunting cheetah cannot withdraw his claws. Therefore, he is not, as are the leopard, the lion, tiger or even our ordinary domestic cat, truly cat-like. Cheetahs live on the ground and cannot climb trees, and their speed and special anatomical structure place them in a class apart.

British term, 'black cotton soil'. The vehicle veered from side to side. The rear wheels tried to go forward and the front ones in the opposite direction. It reminded me of a road covered with black ice. The splashing water in the headlamps was a remarkable sight but, at the same time, it also extinguished all vision. Visibility deteriorated so much that we just could not find the track that would take us to Dr Sachs. 'You are sure to see it,' the German biologist had told us when we met him a fortnight earlier somewhere on Kamaanga island, Lake Victoria. 'It would be such a joy to me if you just turned up at my encampment. You could spend the night and see how I work.' That invitation had been accepted, but there was no trace of the enormous fever-tree to the left of the road nor the track which, after crossing the Grumetti River, would lead to his settlement.

It was now nearly eleven o'clock and, thank goodness, the rain had stopped. Gordon stopped the engine. 'That river must be somewhere near,' he muttered between his teeth. 'Let's investigate.' I was immediately prepared to start searching. I leapt out of the car and not three seconds later I was sitting on my behind. 'Cotton-soil ?' said Gordon with a grin which I bitterly, but silently, resented. 'Cotton my feet,' I growled as I crawled upright. But I was nearly felled for a second time by the slimy surface. Then I could hear it : the river. The abundant rain had changed the dry river-bed into a roaring torrent, which dragged huge branches and complete tree-trunks with it.

It was my turn to triumph : I had discovered the river ! We found a way through, we stumbled through the water and were nearly washed away, but finally we climbed the very slippery bank, kicking stones and mud in all directions.

After having turned round twice in order to avoid mud pools in which we nearly drowned, we saw in the distance a swinging light. It was the German doctor who had seen our headlamps and was now showing us the way.

The greetings were muddy but hearty. Never in my life have I seen a vehicle with a thicker coating of mud than our Land-Rover. We would need a spade to remove it all. However, after our third whisky and a lovely hot goulash made of waterbuck-antelope our miseries were forgotten.

Soon, below a bright starry sky, we were happily playing cards around the camp fire. Near by a lion roared and in the distance we heard the lamenting howls of the hyenas calling each other.

A mother cheetah returns to her young with a young gazelle. Cheetahs kill only for food.

The eland (Taurotragus oryx), *the largest and heaviest of the African antelopes. A bull can weigh up to 2,200 pounds (1,000 kilogrammes). His meat is considered the tastiest of all the grass eaters. Great efforts are being made to turn this species of antelope into a domestic animal whose protein can supply a hungry population.*

1

2. 3 and 4. The nyala (Tragelaphus angasi). *As with most spiral-horned antelopes (including the greater and the lesser kudu, sitatunga and bushbuck), the females are much smaller, without horns and are lighter in colour. This is very obvious with the nyala which I photographed at Mkuze in Natal at a drinking-place. The much longer hair or manes, which the males often have on their necks and backs, plays an important part during the mating display.*

2
3

5. The lesser kudu (Tragelaphus imberbis) *mainly inhabits the dry areas covered with thorny bushes in the* bundu *and the hills of East Africa.*

4
5

Antelopes
Large and small

6

6. *The greater kudu* (Tragelaphus strepsiceros), *with his enormous screw-shaped horns, is one of the most beautiful antelopes. Only in Natal-Zululand could I get him into focal range. Since the great cattle plague at the end of the last century he has become rare in East Africa.*
Bottom photograph : females of the greater kudu.

Rûdiger Sachs is a veterinary surgeon with a special mission in Serengeti. He shoots every zebra, antelope, warthog or buffalo which he catches in his gun-sights at the request of and with special subsidies from the German Government. One cannot help wondering whether, instead of importing European hoofed animals into Africa to breed cattle by our methods in order to feed the hungry and protein-starved African population, it would not be better to use the available species which appear to be suitable for the purpose. Not only have they been accustomed to the environment for a very long time and learned to survive the sometimes extremely difficult food shortages, they have become resistant to the many parasitical diseases.

7. *The roan antelope* (Hippotragus equinus) *belongs to the species of horse antelopes. After the eland and the large kudu it is the largest of the antelopes. The females also have horns.*

8. *The Sitatunga antelope* (Tragelaphus spekei). *Their hooves – clearly visible in the bottom photo of a young specimen – are up to 4 inches (10 centimetres) long, and, as necessary for life in marshland as in water, they can be spread wide apart to make movement across marshy ground safe. The best places to study this rare antelope, previously near Entebbe, is now the Saiwa swamp near Kitale, Kenya.*

10. *The East African oryx* (Oryx gazella beisa), *above, living from Eritrea all the way to the River Tana in Kenya, is fairer in colour and has no tuft of hair at the ears such as his kindred species the Oryx beisa callotis (below), which can be found from the River Tana to within Tanzania. The horns of the oryx are also long and dangerous weapons, for which even lions have great respect. The oryx can go without water for a long time in extremely dry regions. During the day his body temperature rises – a mechanism which enables him not to lose moisture through sweating.*

9

10

English experts have established that, although lacking fat, the African meat has a much higher calorific value than the meat from our slaughterhouses. The buffalo, the warthog and various large antelopes could provide a welcome and ample contribution in protein.

'Look over here,' said the thirty-five-year old bachelor doctor, 'they are full of them,' and with tweezers he drew a 4 inch (10 centimetre) worm from between the skin and flesh of a gnu antelope hanging from a hook in his laboratory. The young veterinarian is instructed to study the suitability of the various varieties of meat. It is generally known, for example, that zebras with a well-fed and very healthy appearance are alive, inside, with maggots. Waterbuck and kongoni have a sour taste, but eland-steak is cherished as a luxury food in East Africa. The recently independent African States with, usually, an underfed population, want to use this livestock which is so rich in protein. Why starve when thousands of antelopes jump about freely in the national parks and nature reserves ?

Tourism, which is now the third largest source of State income, may fill the coffers but certainly not the stomachs of the aboriginal population. Some governments have called in the aid of foreign experts to investigate whether some 'cropping' can be usefully done. There are some precedents already. In Uganda, for example, dozens of zebras were killed every Friday by professional hunters in the Murchison national park. Cropping the surplus of these animals, which owing to their numbers threatened to destroy the food base for other grazers, restores the balance. The meat is sold to the population at reasonable prices. Cropping is now also practised in Tanzania and Zambia. Elephants, buffaloes and hippopotami became victims of this modern and efficient manner of maintaining the African wildstock. The future will show whether this is the right method.

Some twenty Africans skin, hack and put the meat, which has been checked by Sachs, into tins. The tins are stacked with true German thoroughness into neat little rows, ready to be packed and shipped to the German specialised laboratories. There, further investigations will be carried out to establish whether the various meats are germ-free, bacteriologically infected or unsuitable for human consumption.

1. The white-bearded wilde beest or gnu, (Connochaetes taurinus albojubatus). *It is a breathtaking spectable when herds of sometimes hundreds of thousands of animals graze and spread across the Serengeti Plain.*

2, 3 and 4. Impala (Aepyceros melampus). *Known for his enormous leaps of up to 30 feet (10 metres), the impala is the champion of jumping antelopes. The horned bucks sometimes keep a harem herd of forty females.*

1

5. Coke's hartebeest or kongoni (Alcelaphus buselaphus cokii) *another cow antelope, endowed with tremendous endurance.*

6. Sable antelope (Hippotragus niger). *In Rhodesia and South Africa, where I met him, he was known by the name 'Swartwitpens'. The very pugnacious males often fight among themselves.*

7. Blesbok (Damaliscus dorcas philipsi albifrons). *Practically extinct and to be found only in South Africa.*

6

2

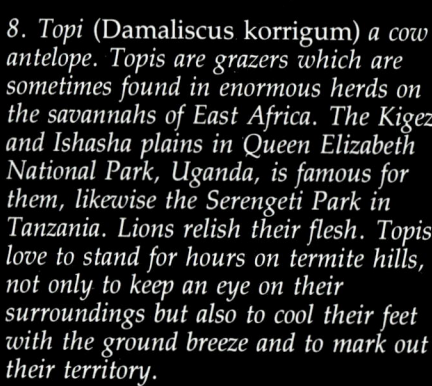
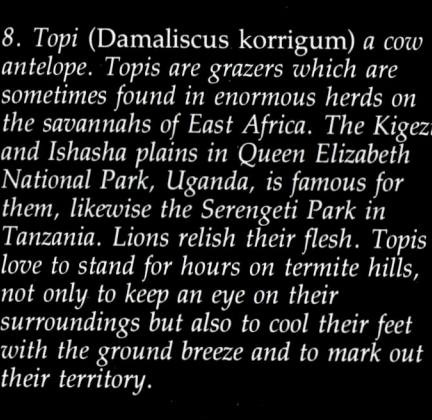

8. Topi (Damaliscus korrigum) *a cow antelope. Topis are grazers which are sometimes found in enormous herds on the savannahs of East Africa. The Kigezi and Ishasha plains in Queen Elizabeth National Park, Uganda, is famous for them, likewise the Serengeti Park in Tanzania. Lions relish their flesh. Topis love to stand for hours on termite hills, not only to keep an eye on their surroundings but also to cool their feet with the ground breeze and to mark out their territory.*

3

7

4

5

8

Defassa-waterbuck (Kobus ellipsiprymnus defassa). *Only the males of these antelopes have strongly ringed horns.*

The British say about the common waterbuck (Kobus ellipsiprymnus ellipsiprymnus) *that it looks as if it has been sitting on a freshly painted lavatory seat!*

Gerenuk, Waller's or giraffe gazelle. This gazelle lives in semi-desert. It has an extremely long neck and, owing to especially mobile hips, the ability to reach the highest branches of the bushes on which it feeds. Generuks never drink; the morning dew on the plants is sufficiant for them.

Uganda kob (Adenota kob thomasi). The male animals have 'arenas' or mating sites : a flattened circular territory which they defend savagely against other males and where only females are permitted. See also page 94.

Family portrait of father, mother and young Thomas's Kob, or Uganda kob, by the Nile.

Bohor reedbuck (Redunca redunca), an antelope, with short horns curving forward, always to be found close to water. They lie up among reed beds or bush during the heat of the day, and graze in the early morning and at dusk.

Oribi (Ourebia ourebia), *one of the steenbok antelopes. They do not like the dry regions very much and often inhabit open downs and low scrubby bush. Their alarm signal is a shrill whistle.*

The red duiker (Cephalophus harveyi) belongs to the species of forest duikers. The bearers of my Scottish friend's name can be found only in tropical rain forests. Photo top right.

The dik-dik antelope (Rhynchotragus kirki hindei) is one of the dwarf antelopes. Some sub-species have an elongated snout, which resemble a little probosis. They are slightly taller than a hare, elegant and gracious in their movements and can be found anywhere in the nyika. *They are peculiar to dense bush country.*

The klipspringer (Oreotragus oreotragus). With their specially formed hooves (as in the European chamois) they are able to climb the steepest of rock faces. Often to be found on kopjes, where they stand guard for hours on end.

Gazelles

Some of the most gracious and beautiful antelopes are called gazelle, which comes from an Arabic word. Antelopes comes from Latin and Greek. Both words mean large eyed.

Grant's gazelle (Gazella granti). Compared to the size of his body the Grant's gazelle has undoubtedly the largest horns of all the antelopes. Some have a length of horn even greater than their shoulder height (photo below).

Peter's gazelle (Gazella granti petersi), in the coastal region above the Tana river, has long erect horns.

Thomson's gazelle *(Gazella thomsoni)*, called 'Tommy' by the British, has a characteristic gait referred to as 'stotting' and an ever-twitching small tail. There are an estimated 500,000 of these charming creatures in the Serengeti. They are the favourite prey of the cheetah.

Seronera

It was six in the morning and still dark when Ngorop, the African boy, coughed beside my mosquito net. *'Hodi ?'* I heard him say. *'Karibu'*, I answered, 'Come in.' 'Tea, Bwana ?' I hate tea, but as a device to help swallowing the anti-malaria pill, it would do.

Ngorop is a genius. It is a pleasure watching him at work around the early morning camp fire. As he pours water to make the tea, his feet are near the fire and between his toes he holds pieces of bread ... he is toasting them !

If you want to see African animals, you have to rise early. The first dawn and the late evening hours are the best, when wild animals go to their drinking places. When the midday sun is high in the sky, they withdraw into the shade unter the brushwood or in the bushes. At this time the vibrant heat, which lingers above the ground as above a hot stove, makes the taking of good photographs impossible. Thinking of all this, I poured a bucket of fresh water over myself, cleaned my teeth and prepared for coming events. We would not eat again until we arrived back at about ten p.m. Surreptitiously I put one of those amazing small red bananas in my mouth; bananas which, like ripe pears, make the juice run over your chin. They have no resemblance at all to the refrigerator-ripened, green products, which taste of flour and dryness.

All around nature was awakening. The rain cuckoo was singing his monotonous song. Yellow-billed hornbills, and splendid glossy starlings were hopping over the ground with great zest searching for insect delicacies.

The European roller (Coracius garrulus), *which used to be an (admittedly displaced) migrant to western Europe, now increasingly prefers the African steppes and their abundance of insects.*

In the still, cool morning air, I stood erect in our Land-Rover with the roof opened up. Within the hour the African sun would strike as a leaden hammer, then it would be better to search for shade, but standing erect in the van with body and head protruding, the sense of surrounding nature was quite acute and I was sniffing merrily the distinctive smells of the forest. Above me vervet monkeys fled away into the high tree-tops, screaming. Helmeted guinea fowl, producing an equally penetrating sound, ran in front of the car. Only at the very last moment, when the car was nearly upon them, did they noisily fly up and then land down again in the bushes. Around us was a galaxy of colour. Bright lilac-breasted rollers, cinnamon-chested bee-eaters and emerald green turacos, red-headed weavers, grey marsh harriers, red and yellow barbets, black cap warblers, nightjars, green wood hoopoes, bearded woodpeckers, or black coucals, all leading to utter confusion ...

With a wide movement another marabou swept down from the sky. Some two hundred had now assembled and I wondered what the large concentration of these birds here in the middle of the Serengeti could mean. I was so intrigued by the spectacle and so busy filming it that the exclamation of Gordon 'It's a kill' and the accompanying push in the ribs threw me off balance.

I was no longer sitting on the seat but next to it when Gordon Harvey like a Formula One racing driver accelerated full throttle and joltingly drove in the opposite direction. The marabous were chased up into the air by the

When the lilac-breasted roller (Coracius caudata) leaves his vantage point and takes to his wing, he looks like a flying jewel.

An extraordinary collection of marabou storks in the Grumeti corridor, Serengeti, Tanzania.

As soon as the hunting dogs (above) have had their fill, the spotted hyenas (below) appear on the scene.

sudden noise. Immediately I could see it all. A troop of hunting dogs had started stalking a herd of gnu-antelopes wilde beest. With one leg still in the air and my cameras as far as possible removed from all the ironwork, I got up and tried to assess the situation. Gordon was now on a level with the galloping animals. Following their usual tactic of taking it in turns, the wild dogs had separated one of the gnus from the herd. As a chased antelope will always run in a wide circle, it cannot possibly hold out against the co-operating brigands and will finally fall to the terror of the pack.

After some ten minutes this stage had been reached. The exhausted animal stood still, breathing heavily. For a little while it tried to defend itself with head butts and hoof kicks against the in-rushing, fresh pack, but nothing could save it from the ruthless carnivores. Two of the beasts of prey held on to the tail, whilst others bit into the soft underbelly of the poor animal.

Although we were now less than 20 yards (20 metres) away, the excited beasts were unperturbed by our presence. The random yellow, black and white spotted killers jumped yelping and howling, around their victim which had now fallen to its knees. After a few minutes the animal was dead and some twenty-five hunting dogs tore bloody pieces of flesh from it. The cruel law of nature in which one animal devours the other in order to live had worked once more. We had now approached to within 5 yards (5 metres). Growling and yelping, the wild beasts were surrounding their prey, their enormous ears and blood-dripping muzzles turned in our direction. Would they leave their victim in order to concentrate on the iron monster ? Their hunger took precedence, although they kept a close eye on us. From all around vultures approached, to fly in wide circles over the scene of slaughter. The marabous also came closer, then suddenly there was panic.

Two hyenas, appearing on the scene, crept quietly near but were chased away by the pack. Next, three black-backed jackals came closer by. The entire cleansing department of the African plains was present. Half an hour later little more than half was left of the cow-sized gnu. By dusk there would not be much more than the carcass and the skull. During the night, the hyenas would crack the bones and the ants would finish the rest.

There was one antelope less on the Serengeti plain, but some gnu females lay near by with their new-born young. Life goes on.

The hunting dog, or African wild dog, (Lycaon pictus). Their social life has been extensively studied and described by J. and H. von Lawick-Goodall and other zoologists.

Leopards
and other pirates

The best place in Africa to find leopards is along the Seronera River in Tanzania. At night they go into the surrounding plains to hunt. During daytime, they sleep, perfectly camouflaged, in some fever-tree or Acacia, or they search in the early morning for the first warming rays of the sun on the koppies. It is usually in these koppies that they give birth to their young or where they cleverly hide themselves between fissures in the rocks. With a little luck, and a great deal of patience, these large cats can be watched quenching their thirst at the riverside (photo below right).

The leopard (*Panthera pardus*) is a solitary animal. Only during mating time are they seen in mature couples. The young cubs remain with their mother for quite a long time – sometimes until they are adults. During the last thirty years the numbers of leopards have been greatly reduced – because of fur coats : a whim of fashion. Fortunately, a number of countries including, in 1971, the United States have forbidden the importation of the skins of the spotted cats.

Leopards are specialists in unexpected attack. After long and patient stalking, they leap onto their prey at the last moment. Their menu is the most varied in the animal world. They kill and feed on all the antelope species, rock-dassies, baboons, guinea-fowl, bat-eared foxes and even pythons. Many a farmer's dog, however large or small, has disappeared when a leopard was near by.

The serval (*Leptailurus serval*) a small, spotted beast of prey, is seldom to be seen. He is hunted for his skin, but, like most spotted cats, he hunts only at night and hides during the day in the thickest bushes. His extremely large ears, touching each other at the front of his skull, serve him well when searching for mice and rats. The typical white mirrors on the ears are guides for offspring, which can follow the parent through the high grass by watching them. Photos below and right.

1. *The caracal or African lynx (Caracal caracal).* An occupant of the thorn-bush savannahs which feeds on rodents, klipspringers, dik-diks, young gazelles and impalas. The caracal can live in peace for the time being. Why ? His pelt is not spotted and as such is quite worthless for the fur trade.

2. *The bat-eared fox (Otocyon megalotis)* is known by his enormous ears and his very special set of teeth : some fifty of them - very good for eating insects and his favourite food, termites and migratory locusts. He also includes small birds and eggs in his diet.

3. *The black-backed jackal (Canis mesomelas)* lives mainly on what is left by lions and hyenas. Is often found near calving antelopes, when he will devour the newly born young and the after-birth.

4. *The golden, common jackal (Canis aureus),* the nearest relation of the wolf. Together with the hyena he belongs to the cleansing brigade of the African savannahs, but on occasion he falls victim himself (5).

1

2

3

4

5

Hyenas

The spotted hyena (Crocuta crocuta germinans) *could be called the chief of the public cleansing department. His strong teeth (the strongest in the animal world) can crack the largest bones. Together with vultures, jackals, marabous and other carrion eaters, he cleans the African desert of all rotting carcasses. He is also a killer of ungulates.*

The hyenas howled without interruption. There is no place in Africa where these animals have such audacity as in the Serengeti corridor in Tanzania. Camping in the Ngorongoro crater – where one can follow them on their trails even during daytime – I had already had some experience with animals of prey, which are often so wrongly called 'carrion eaters'.

After a simple evening meal and a chat around the dying camp-fire, we had settled down for the night. A five o'clock rise in the morning encourages one to go to bed early. As usual, I had left the flaps of my tent open to get whatever air or wind there was. Gordon had put his camp-bed underneath a schermacacia and had fixed his mosquito-net to an overhanging branch. His snoring was in harmony with the nearby menacingly tittering-growling and howling of the hyenas. Natural background sounds in this environment do not disturb my sleep. The song of the crickets, the chirping of the thousands of cicadas, are sounds which belong to a camp in the African wilderness. You have to get used to the croaking of the hundreds of tree-frogs and blow-frogs, the sometimes electric sounds of the nightjar, the penetrating howling of the tree *Hyrax*, the distant roar of the lion or the heavy 'sawing' of the leopard. When camping by a river, you must be prepared for the bellowing of the hippos, the cries of frightened geese or the lightly sleeping baboons in the surrounding trees, the sad monotonous cry of the thick-knees and other plovers. One gets used to it, and it certainly adds variety to the environment.

Having been up since before five a.m. and after a heavy day, I surely would have been fast asleep had I not been disturbed by unusually heavy snoring of my Scottish friend. With frowned eyebrows and a warning look in my left eye I stared in the moonlight at the white, shining mosquito-net from which direction the Scottish sound, which had little to do with bagpipe music, emerged.

Suddenly both my eyes opened wide. At the bottom of my bed, *inside* the tent, stood a hyena which appeared to be enormous. It was looking around for something to eat and had lowered its head inside my shoes. I did not hesitate for a moment. I did not use my nightlamp to shine on the intruder; I threw it with all my might. With a soul-destroying howl the beast stormed out of my tent – accompanied by a few Flemish swear-words and a few shouts in Gordon's direction. Sitting upright on his camp-bed, with a rather stupid look on his face, Gordon stared aghast at the hyena racing past him, with hair standing upright and followed by everything I could lay my hands on, an empty beer bottle, a shaving brush, an over-ripe mango, a toothbrush and a safari shoe. The shoe I recaptured immediately after the nervous giggling of the hyena had died away in the distance.

It reminded me how a tame young hyena, who was running around freely amongst the other pets of the late Armand Denis in Langata, Nairobi, had escaped with my leather camera case, whilst I was photographing. It was quite a job, aided by Armand Denis and his African helpers to convince the young rascal to give up his captured booty. Although I proudly carry around a camera-holster showing hyena teethmarks, I would not like a real wild hyena to escape with my safari boots.

I was very grateful to Gordon for producing such loud snoring that night. Otherwise I would not have seen the hyena enter my tent, and the remainder of my safari would have been made on bare feet or with one shoe … which gives food for thought in this thorny land.

SERONERA, TANZANIA

Our encampment in the Ngorongoro crater in Tanzania, the best place in Africa to arrange an encounter with Fisi, the hyena. I witnessed in broad daylight a herd of zebras being chased by a troop of hyenas.

My tent in the Serengeti Plain in Tanzania, where I was visited by a hyena during the night.

A young hyena on exploration in the Rwindi Plain in Zaire

Before starting their nightly scavenging two adult hyenas greet each other near Kasese in Uganda.

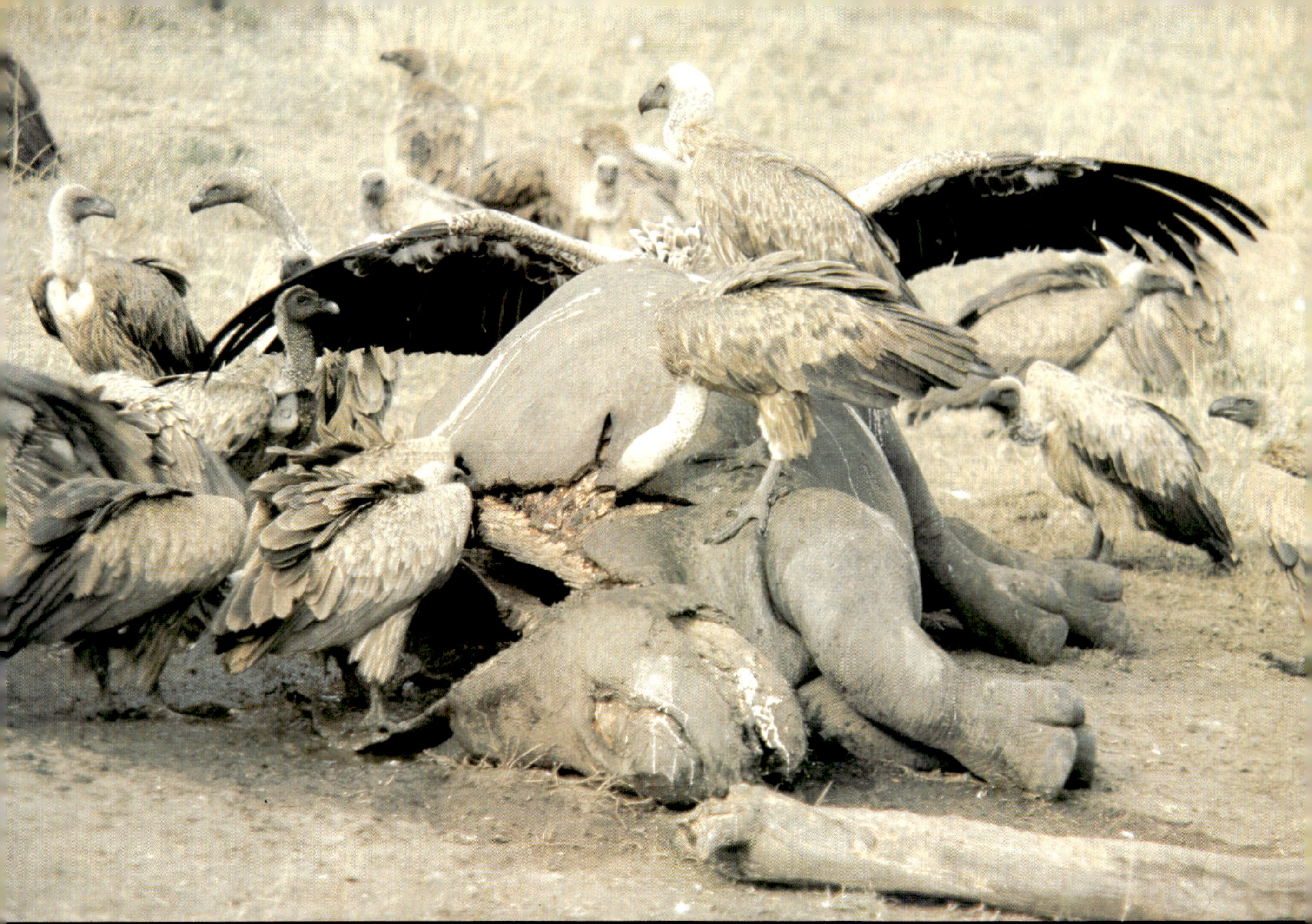

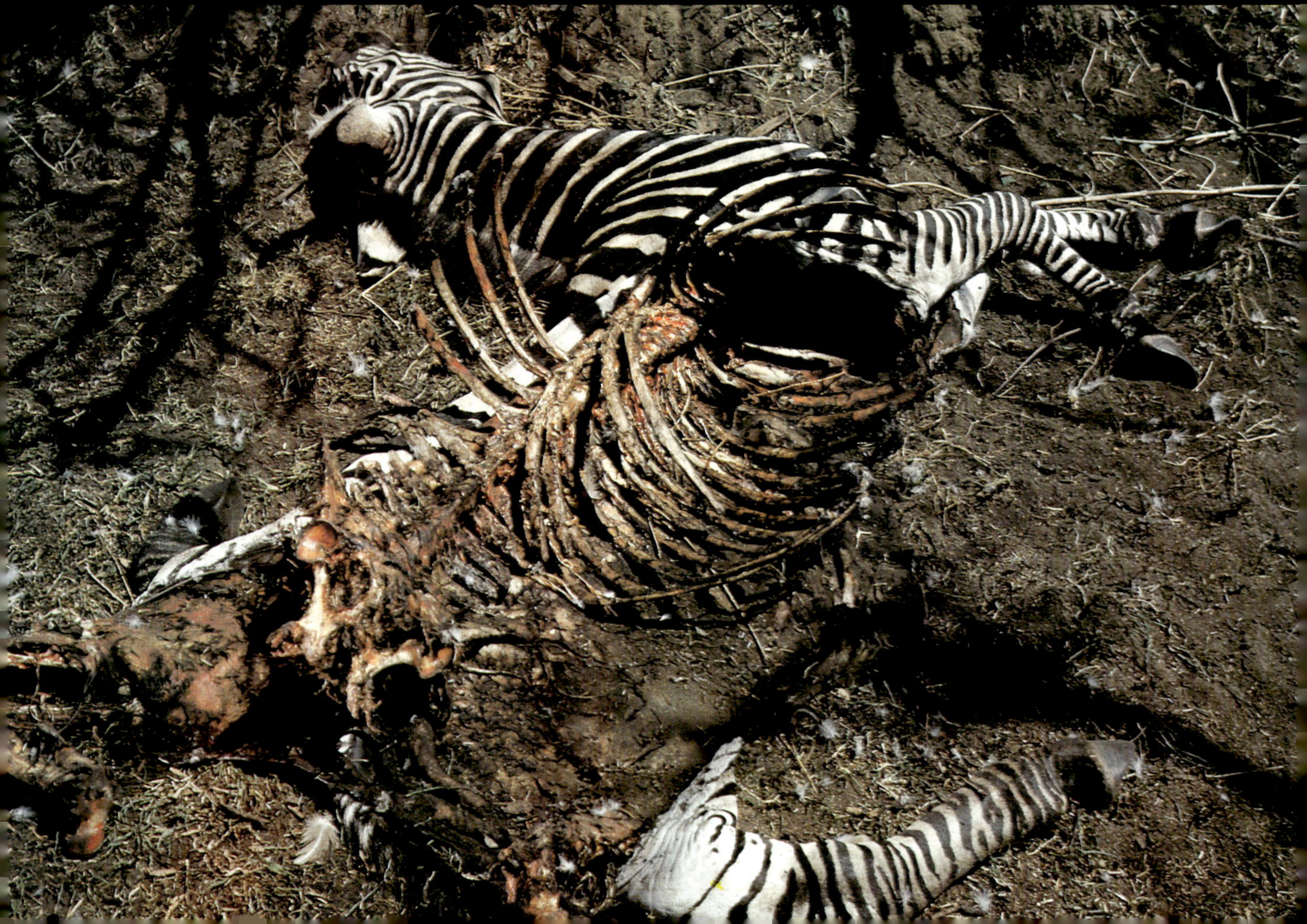

The cleansing service of Africa

The cleansing service of Africa may repel some people. Despite their unappetising eating habits, and their dismal menu, the animals performing this task are extremely useful and their hygienic work is indispensable. Animals which have died of disease, rotting carcasses and half-eaten carrion are promptly dealt with. Thanks to them, epidemics are kept under control. From an ecological point of view they are most important.

Vultures, who frequently appear on these pages, with their powerful beaks and aided by their heavy claws, can tear asunder the skin of large animals, such as rhinos (see top photo page 108), elephants or zebras. The long featherless neck of these large birds enables them to penetrate deep within the carcasses of dead animals without making their feathers dirty.

Of note is the special 'radar' used by the vultures when searching for carrion. As soon as a cheetah or lion has made a kill, vultures appear on the scene, although, at the time, none could be seen in the sky. Somewhere very high up there must have been a vulture, who dived down as soon as he spotted something. A neighbour, gliding some distance away, must have seen or heard him dive and followed suit, and so on. Sometimes, hundreds of vultures are to be seen peacefully awaiting their turn until the large predators have satisfied their hunger. Then suddenly the cleansing service goes into full action. Hyenas, jackals, marabous, vultures, kites and ravens join in, until only a patch of congealed blood remains. This will be finally cleared away by ants or other insects.

Page 108, above : White-backed vultures (Pseudogyps ruppellii) *devour a rhinoceros killed by poachers in Kenya.*
Page 108 below : The cleansing department has finished its job.
On this page :
Above left : Hooded vulture (Necrosyrtes monachus), *a completely omnivorous all-devouring creature.*
Above right : Egyptian vulture (Neophron percnopterus).
Centre : left; immature Ruppell's griffon vulture and, right, white-backed vulture (Pseudogyps africanus).

At the bottom of this page : The inseparable hyena and white-backed vultures with a hooded vulture in the foreground.
Photo page 110 : Lapped-faced vulture (Torgos tracheliotus); *one of the largest African vultures.*

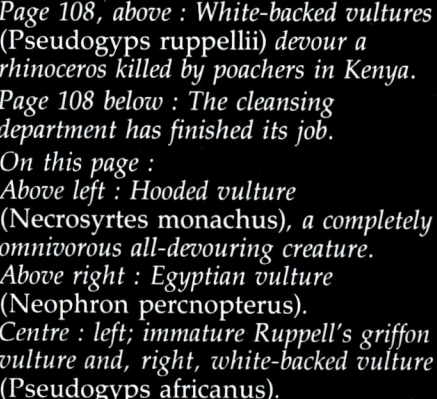

In Kipedo, on the Sudanese-Ugandan border, we found this nest with two dozen ostrich eggs, each egg weighing about 5 1/2 pounds (2 1/2 kilogrammes). The female ostriches, living polygamously, lay all their eggs in the same nest, hence the large numbers. During the daytime the female takes her turn on the nest as her colouring is more protective; at night a male takes over.

Ostriches

Young ostriches (top right) look like their mother; neutral in colour. The males have a contrasting black-and-white suit with, during the mating season, enormous and gorgeous feathers.

The Masai ostrich (Struthio camelus massaicus) has a pink neck, which sometimes turns scarlet during the mating season (centre photo).

The Somali ostrich (Struthio camelus molybdophanes), by contrast, has a blue neck. Weighing some 330 pounds (150 kilogrammes), the ostrich is the largest non-flying bird in the world.

Left : The ground hornbill (Bucorvus leadbeateri cafer) resembles a turkey, his deep growling is like that of a lion. His walk is dignified when he steps through the bush, searching for lizards, snakes and insects. On many an occasion I have seen him turning elephants'excrement over hunting for beetles. The male has a red throat bag; the female's is sometimes blue.

Above right : The black-bellied bustard, called the long-legged black grouse in South Africa, (Eupodotis barrowi in Natal, Lissotis melanogaster in Kenya) is a smaller species of bustard which makes a typical 'pop' sound, similar to a balloon being pricked. This is used as a decoy and contact cry.

Photos below right and above : The kori (Ardeotis kori) in South African gompauw. It weighs about 45 pounds (20 kilogrammes) and is therefore the largest flying bird in Africa. When displaying, the kori changes completely and appears to turn inside out in order to be as impressive as possible. He blows up his large throat bag at the front of his neck, spreads his tail across his back, and suddenly looks like an enormous white ball of feathers.

Three bottom photos on the left : Black-faced sand grouse (Erimialector decoratus) greatly resemble pigeons when in flight. They inhabit extremely dry, desert-like regions. However, as seed-eaters they cannot live without water and therefore have to fly great distances daily – up to 30 miles (50 kilometres) and more – in order to drink. They do this in great flocks and at precise times of the day. When drinking, they dip their breast feathers deep into the water to carry enough to satisfy their thirsty brood upon return to their nests.

Naivasha-Nakuru

The heavenly Lake Naivasha has an astounding variety of birds, there being more than three hundred species, Above, a crown crane accompanied by spoonbills and pelicans.

The purple gallinule (Porphyrio porphyrio) has a very striking appearance with his purple-blue feathers, red forehead, red legs and long toes and is a delight to the eye. I used to see many of them on Lake Naivasha, now they have become much rarer.

Lake Naivasha, one of the few fresh-water lakes in Kenya, was 'discovered' in 1883 by the German naturalist Gustav Fischer, accompanied by a caravan of three hundred carriers. A year later he was followed by Josef Thomson who was promptly killed by a buffalo. At the time Lake Naivasha was inhabited by large numbers of hippos and around it lived elephants, antelopes, giraffes and zebras.

Lake Naivasha similar to Lake Baringo, is also fed by an underground, volcanic catchment supply. Owing to its high location in the Great Rift Valley, it looks cool and moist. The surrounding area is lush and green. The enormous papyrus growths, sometimes forming floating islands and water lillies create an idyllic environment.

Before 1920 Lake Naivasha had very few fish, only the small variety (*Aplocheilechthys antinorii*). In 1926 it was stocked with tilapia in order to combat the dangerous mosquito larvae. A little later the American wide-mouth bass was introduced. Now the lake is rich in fish and large colonies of pelicans feed on the lake.

There is abundance of cormorants, spoonbills, ibis, grebes, kingfishers and terns, all living exclusively on fish. The sound best known to the ears of any safari traveller or visitor to the African lakes is the call of the fish eagle. When the African fish eagle (*Haliaeëtus cuncuma vocifer*) throws his head back – almost down to his back – and produces his cry, resounding far across the water – regularly to be answered by a friend across the lake – he plants a memory which will stay in one's mind for ever. It forms part of the nostalgia of Africa, the constant longing for those heavenly regions, such as Lake Naivasha, Baringo or Nakuru.

Left : An African fish eagle (Haliaeëtus vocifer).

The African Jacana or lily-trotter (Actophilornis africanus). A land-shy bird, usually to be found on the water-lilies, where he dexterously turns the leaves in his search for small snails.

In 1961-2 the water level of the East African lakes rose conspicuously. Many trees were drowned and now exist only to provide excellent nesting places for the cormorants (Phalacrocorax lucidus).

Black crake (Limnocorax flavirostra) searching for insects on Salvinia algae. The bird is entirely black except for his apple-green beak and pinky-red legs.

The African darter (Anhinga rufa). A bird, living near fresh water, but in many respects similar to the cormorant. The head and the craned thin neck are above the water when he swims and gives him his name. An excellent spear fisher. The northern end of Gibraltar – an island in Lake Baringo – centre photo – is a well-known breeding place for anhingas.

Cormorants and darters hunt their prey below the water's surface. Although they grease their feathers with a substance from the coccyx, their feathers are not waterproof and have to be dried in the sun.

Cormorants have a hooked beak by which they grip their prey and hold on to it. Anhingas do not catch their prey but spear it with their long and sharp beak.

Contrary to Lake Naivasha, which is a fresh-water lake, Lake Nakuru is an alkaline salt-water lake.

During some seasons up to two million flamingoes *(Phoenicepterus ruber)* can be seen on Lake Nakuru; that is two thirds of the flamingoes living in Africa, half of the world population (photo below).

The little grebes or dabchicks *(Poliocephalus ruficollis)*, a dwarf great-crested grebe which feeds on underwater vegetation. Suddenly he vanished only to appear again like a small ball up to 35 yards (20-30 metres) farther away. Photo below left.

Large sections of Lake Naivasha used to be covered with pink water-lilies (two photos below). Few water-lilies remain owing to recent introduction of fresh-water crayfish which have eliminated them.

White pelicans (Pelecanus onocrotalus). However clumsy they are on the ground, with their wings out-stretched to a span of 9 feet (2.7 metres), they suddenly become extremely powerful and most elegant gliders. Floating on the rising hot-air currents, they can stay aloft for hours on end. They are social birds, hunting for fish in groups, catching them after driving them together in shoals, and quite effortlessly retaining them in their spoon-like lower beak.

Around 1968 the first rodent-like coypus (Myocaster coypus) appreared in Lake Naivasha. Nobody knows how this South American animal came here. Probably they escaped from a fur farm (their skin is called nutria). Their main food consists of vegetable matter, mainly reeds and waterplants. Like the Salvinia algae and the crayfish they are destroying the balanced ecology of Lake Naivasha.

The smallest of the African ducks : the blue-billed Hottentot teal (Anas punctata). For its name alone I wanted to include it in in this book, here seen together with the red-billed duck (Anas erythrorhyncha)).

The white-faced tree duck (Dendrocygna viduata) feeds on grass seeds and water plants. He is most active at night and his whistling is a typical night sound along the large lakes.

The black-winged stilt (Himantopus himantopus) has the longest legs of all the birds on earth compared to its body size. It feeds on all sorts of water insects and on mosquito larvae. It is a cosmopolitan bird with many sub-species all over the world (bottom left).

Lesser flamingoes (Phoeniconaias minor) with pelicans. Left foreground, a marsh sandpiper (Tringa stagnatilis). They all live and hunt together, each species searching for and finding its specific food.

The marabou (Leptoptilos crumeniferus) *belongs to the stork family. Although it can be found in Africa along the rivers and on the banks of lakes, its reputation as carrion eater and omnivore is well known. Its enormous wedge-shaped beak guarantees a place of honour at any sizeable carcass. Marabous live on crocodile eggs, rats, frogs, lizards, locusts, carrion and even human excrement. Their motto : variety is the spice of life !*

Much more elegant is the little egret (Egretta garzetta). The slow movement of its yellow toes under water attracts the fishes which he then gulps down.

(Photo bottom right and on the next page) : Black-headed heron (Ardea melanocephala).

The majestic saddle-bill stork (Ephippiorhynchus senegalensis) has its name because it seems to walk about with a saddle on its beak. It is the largest of the storks in Africa. The male has dark brown eyes, the female yellow.

The African grey heron (Ardea cinerea) stands patiently on guard for hours on end until a fish passes by …

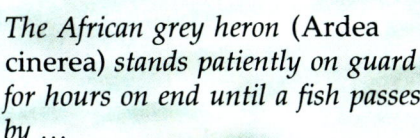

The goliath heron (Ardea goliath), 5 feet (1.5 metres) tall, is the largest of the herons. Its slow-motion beating of the wings in flight is a beautiful sight to see.

The little egret (Egretta garzetta)) whose yellow socks we have mentioned already. Later on we shall look at their numbers.

Two photos above right : The yellow-billed stork or wood-ibis, (Ibis ibis) above right, together with a white-necked cormorant, is a true stork and not, in fact an ibis. During the breeding season his face mask becomes blood red. The wood-ibis hunts for frogs and fishes and is considered to be the bird with the fastest reflexes in the world.

Two photos bottom right :
A number of legends surround the hammerkop (Scopus umbretta). No African would dare to tempt providence with this bird as it could cause instant misfortune. And whoever falls under the shadow of one flying over head may expect a death in the family the same day. This stork-like creature – because that is what it is – builds enormous nests, which can support a grown-up man and which contain various rooms. Investigators have established that it requires more than 8,000 branches and twiglets to make a nest which is completed in about six months or longer.

Left top : the great white egret (Casmerodius albus) searching for food (see also the facing page). The bird's decorative feathers were very fashionable at the turn of the century and whole colonies were exterminated, while millions of pounds were made at the height of the fashion in London by the sale of the feathers which were worth their weight in gold. Fortunately, the 'aigrettes' fell from fashion and the breed was re-established.

Left : second photo from above : The buff-backed heron or cattle egret (Ardeola or Bubulcus ibis) can always be found near large animals : elephants, buffaloes or rhinos. They literally follow the foodsteps of anything grazing, picking up disturbed insects as they go.

Third photo from top left :
The hadada ibis (Hagedashi hagedashi) draws attention by its loud, unmistakable cry. Hence the English name 'hadada' – an onomatopoeia or sound imitation. He belongs to the same family as the sacred ibis (Threskiornis aethiopica), photo to the right, which for some 5,000 years has been associated with the culture of mankind. Pictures of the ibis can be found in the tombs of the Egyptian pharaohs. However, even in that country (oh ! civilisation !) it is now becoming a great rarity.

Photos below :
The squacco heron (Ardeola ralloides) waits with incredible patience until a fish swims by, while the sacred ibis with its bent beak ploughs through the mud and the wood-ibis treads through the water with wide-open beak. All hunt in their different ways for food which is abundantly available in the African lakes.

The extremely elegant black-winged stilt (see also page 121) can be found in Ndumu, on the border with Mozambique, where it steps confidently past a crocodile, as well as on the banks of the enormous Lake Turkana in north Kenya.

The spur or blacksmith plover (*Hoplopterus armatus*) not only got its name from the spurs on its wings, but also because its call resembles a hammer beating an anvil. It is the alarm clock of the African river banks; warning both large and small animals when there is danger on the waterfront.

The avocet (*Recu... ...avosetta*), with its blue legs and up-turned beak, can scoop insects, molluscs and small lobsters from the mud. It can be found near the banks of Lake Naivasha, Nakuru or Elmentaita. It breeds regularly at Lake Magadi.

Africa on stilts

The African wattled plover, *(Afribyx senegallus)*. I did not always find this bird near water, but sometimes far inland (photo above). Just like a collector of cigar bands or stamps, I feel justly proud of having recorded on film practically all the species of plovers in East Africa.

The stone curlew or thicknee *(Burhinus vermiculatus)*. The British call him 'dikkop', a name that has come from South Africa. There is also the Cape curlew, or thick-knee, *(Burhinus capensis)*, which can be found in the dry savannah. As with most birds living on the water's edge, the water curlew lays its two eggs usually between stones and branches, where they are perfectly camouflaged by their irregular spot-pattern (centre photo).

Below :
Camping by a stream in Africa, one can be sure of hearing, during the night, the distinctive alarm cry of this bird. Together with the cicadas, the night-jars, bats, frogs and toads they form the chorus of night life.

On the other page :
More than six hundred million migrant birds escape the European winter every year to go to Africa. Plovers, snipes, ruffs, sandpipers, greenshanks – all come from the Siberian tundra or western Europe in order to pass the winter here. Top left : Ruff (Philomachus pugnax), never in breeding-plumage in Africa, and the wood sandpiper (Tringa glareola). The latter bred with us until 1936.
(Right) : Little stints (Calidris minuta) come all the way from Siberia and Scandinavia to pass the winter here.

(Centre photos) : Wood sandpipers (Tringa glareola). Sacred ibis (bottom photo), lesser black-backed gulls (Larus fuscus)), grey-headed gulls (Larus cirrocephalus) and spurwing plovers at the tide mark of Lake Turkana.

On this page :
The extraordinary grace of the elegant crowned crane (Balearica pavonina) (above), with golden crown and decorative colouring varying from the most delicate grey to brownish red and blue, takes one's breath away. The top feathers of the under-tail of the African marabou (below) are extremely soft and fluffy and were at one time very popular in the world of fashion. That is why this member of the African cleansing department has become relatively rare.

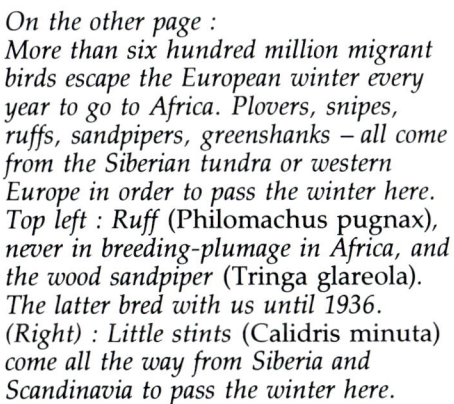

1.2. *If the pied kingfisher (Ceryle rudis) is not sitting on his look-out perch, then he is suspended above the water's surface prepared to dive like a torpedo into the water. The prey, usually a small fish, is first killed against a branch and then swallowed down head first. The male differs from the female by its supplementary band across its chest.*

3. *The giant kingfisher (Megaceryle maxima) can seldom be seen. The diet of this timid bird consists mainly of fish, fresh water crabs and insects. The pigmy kingfisher (Ispidina picta) and the malachite kingfisher (Alcedo cristata) are flying jewels. Their diet is mainly small fish and water insects.*

Pied kingfishers on the equator

The red-billed hornbill (Tockus erythrorhynchus) has his coverts conspiciously spotted white. It can be found in the thorn bush savannah.

In Kenya alone there are some 1,035 different species of birds, more than 1,400 in Kenya, Uganda and Tanzania. If one compares this to the 577 in Europe one realises that Africa can rightly be called a birds' paradise.

As in our country, the most remarkable singers (nightingales, white throats, warblers or flycatchers) have the most undistinguished colouring.

Right : The whinchat (Saxicola rubreta), a European singing bird which spends the winter in Zambia and East Africa.

In Kenya alone there are more than 60 different species of sunbirds (Nectariniidae). With their long, bent, pointed beak and equally long tongue, they know how to get honey from flowers. The male sunbirds have a splendid plumage with areas of metallic, shiny feathers. However, the females are remarkably colourless.

Left : An immature scarlet-chested sunbird (Chalcomitra senegalensis).

The yellow-throated long-claw (Macronyx croceus), combines a not unpleasant song with beautiful plumage and a very long nail on the rear toe.

The white-eyed slatey fly-catcher (Melaenornis chocolatina) is extremely fond of flying ants.

The white-bellied Go-Away-bird, known locally as 'guguku' (Corythaixoides leucogaster), has annoyed many a hunter with its insistent warning cry. Even if one stalks an elephant or rhino with the greatest prudence, suddenly there is the nasal 'go away' of the grey guguku !

When the golden pipit (Tmetothylacus tenellus) is in flight it resembles a bright yellow canary. The British sometimes call it the butterfly bird.

One of the twenty species of woodpeckers in East Africa – the Nubian woodpecker (Campethera nubica).

The violet-eared waxbill (Uraeginthus granatinus), a winged jewel, was kept in a golden cage by the famous mistress of Louis XV, Madame de Pompadour.

The white-throated bee-eater (Aerops àlbicollis).

Besides the European species which pass the winter in Africa, there are dozens of native swallows, one of the most beautiful being the wire-tailed swallow (Hirundo smithii.)

The white-browed coucal, or waterbottle bird, (Centropus superciliosus) is named thus, thanks to its peculiar call. The sound can be heard over a great distance and resembles a bottle being emptied. Although it belongs to the cuckoo family the coucal is not parasitic in its breeding habits.

In Uganda and Rwanda are the northern black-throated weavers (Ploceus castanops) one of the dozens of species of industrious nest-builders with a skill in weaving which astounds ornithologists.

The carmine bee-eater (Merops nubicus). This brilliant red bee-eater is usually found in flocks and also breeds in large colonies.

By virtue of its dull mottled plumage the dusky nightjar (Caprimulgus fraenatus) can camouflage himself perfectly during the day.

The long-tailed fiscal shrike (Lanius cabanisi). As with most shrikes he builds up a stock of prey by impaling beetles, lizards and locusts on thorns.

The little bee-eater (Melittophagus pusillus) came to visit me every day in our encampment on the Uaso-Nyiro River in Kenya.

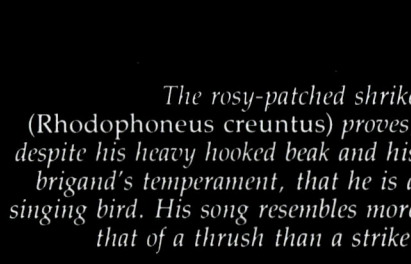

The rosy-patched shrike (Rhodophoneus creuntus) proves, despite his heavy hooked beak and his brigand's temperament, that he is a singing bird. His song resembles more that of a thrush than a strike.

Little bee-eaters in full plumage.

The red and yellow barbet (Trachyphonus erythrocephalus), belongs to the splendid family of 'ground barbets'. The pair make their nest-hole in the ground and they sing in duets.

The red-tailed shrike (Lanius isabellinus) comes from Russian Turkestan and Manchuria to spend the winter in Africa.

The carmine bee-eater (Merops nubicus) is without doubt one of the most beautiful birds in Africa.

The weaver birds (Ploceidae), related to our house sparrows, are known for their cleverly woven nests. When the structure is complete, the male hangs at the entrance and by revolving movements and beating of wings invites, with a lot of noise, his beloved to come and inspect his masterpiece.

Turacos

I cannot hide my deep admiration for the turacos, which I consider to be among the most striking, most beautiful and most interesting birds of the African continent. Out of the dozen species I would like to mention two of which I am particularly fond. The *Ross's tauraco*, the discovery of which reminds one of a fairy tale, and the blue-crested Hartlaub's turaco *(Tauraco hartlaubi)* (photo left).

Patrick Ross who was the governor of the island of St Helena, often travelled to Africa, Angola, Benguela, the Congo and Uganda bringing back presents from his journeys for Lady Ross, his wife, a woman of rare beauty. Amongst them was a live bird of exotic colouring. Lady Ross kept this bird for ten years in her aviary on the island of St Helena. When the bird died, in 1854, she sent its cured skin to the great British ornithologist Gould. As this species of touracos was unknown until then, Gould

gave it the name Lady Ross's turaco *(Musophaga rossae)*.

Thanks to Tim Barnley I was able to film the Lady Ross in the forest around the Saiwa swamp near Kitale in Kenya. Although they are difficult to observe in the forest greenery, due to their protective colouring, they are like a red flame flashing through the forest when suddenly they fly away. Their bright red touracine-coloured wings are real fireworks. The cry of the Hartlaub turacos, inseparably bound up with my encampments in the Aberdare mountains of Kenya or on the slopes of Mt Kilimanjaro in Tanzania, together with the cry of the fish eagle and the mournful call of the crowned cranes, are sounds which always make me yearn for tropical Africa.

Birds of prey

Besides the majestic fish eagle which we described on page 114 (photo left), there are quite a number of birds of prey in Africa – the long-crested hawk eagle (Lophoaëtus occipitalis) for example, (to the right). This black-brown rough-legged hawk feeds almost exclusively on rodents, rats and mice.

The martial eagle (Polemaëtus bellicosus) has a less pronounced tuft, yet he can boast of being the largest African eagle.

Photo below :
However, the real reptile destroyer is the secretary bird or snake eagle (Sagittarius serpentarius). He stalks unremittingly through the high grass, catching snakes or lizards behind the head with his long, powerful claws and swallowing them down in one gulp.

Without doubt, Africa is the land of birds of prey; nowhere in the world have I seen such a variety. To the great numbers of sparrow-hawks, hawks, kites, falcons, buzzards and marsh harriers, there can be added fourteen different species of eagles which can be found in Africa. Nine of them are local residents, the other five come from Europe and Asia just to spend the winter here.

One of Africa's most beautiful birds of prey is probably the Bateleur (Terathopius ecaudatus) *which also belongs to the family of snake eagles. It earned its name from its acrobatic tricks. In the mating period the male performs real circus acts in the air. Sometimes he can be seen passing the prey to his female when in full flight. With his extremely short tail he has a characteristic flight which is hard to forget. He has an extremely large territory and lives on reptiles and carrion (large photo left).*

In north-east Kenya, at the border of Somaliland, an almost white specimen of the steppe eagle can be seen. In the thorn savannah it is hard to differentiate between the steppe eagle and the tawny eagle.

A couple of tawny eagles (Aquila rapax), *(below), sometimes used the same nest year after year, to which they added extensions (photo page 140 below).*

Not far away from the heavenly Lake Naivasha lies Hell's Gate, an impressive chasm with, on one of the rock ledges at least 330 feet (100 metres) high, the mighty lammergeyer or bearded vulture (Gypaëtus barbatus) nests. Thanks to John G.Williams, the world renowned ornithologist who accompanied me on a few safaris, we could record on film this unique, threatened bird of prey, which has a wingspan of up to 8 1/2 feet (2.80 metres). (See flight photo).

The martial eagle (Polemaëtus bellicosus), is the largest African eagle. It attacks even young antelopes but, for the rest, makes do with monkeys, rock hyrax, small mammals, guinea powl, etc. (photo left top).

The augur buzzard, (Buteo rufofuscus) (photo bottom left), is the most common buzzard in East and South Africa. His jackal-like call resounds over the low hills and the savannah. He is closely related to the eagles, so is the long-crested hawk eagle (Lophoaetus occipitalis) (see flight picture below).

The African black kite (Milvus migrans) is one of the most common birds of prey in Africa. It differs from the European kite by its yellow beak. It is omnivorous and a great acrobat (bottom photo).

The largest African owl is the Verreaux's eagle owl (Bubo lacteus) *(photo page right)*. I have seen it up to 6,500 feet (2,000 metres) high in the Kenya mountains.

Photo above : The spotted eagle owl (Bubo africanus).

There are two species of goshawks (Melierax musicus) in Kenya : the dark chanting goshawk (Melierax metabates) and the pale chanting goshawk (Melierax poliopterus). I was able to film the dark species near the Elgon mountains, and the lighter species at the borders of Somalia. (Photo to the left and left on page 145.)

The smallest African bird of prey without a doubt is the pygmy falcon (Polihierax semitorquatus). It measures barely 7 inches (18 centimetres). It makes its nest in deserted weaver-birds' nests and enjoys a diet of beetles, other insects as well as small lizards and mice (photo page 145 right).

The African jungle at night is unimaginable without owls. However, to get them within range is quite another matter. During the day they are hidden in hollow trees or in between the thickest leaves

The Ngurdoto crater in Tanzania, is an extinct, extensive volcano, down which no man may descend without a special permit. Nature protection is total here and perhaps, in this way, a slice of nature will be preserved intact for posterity. However, one is allowed to penetrate the virgin forest at the upper edge of this strictly guarded sanctuary, and there are even specially built look-outs for tourists. Armed with field glasses it is possible to see the crater floor – where there is always water available – and watch herds of buffaloes, elephants, wart-hogs and three or four different species of monkeys.

On the slopes of the nearby Meru mountain I photographed the elephant that decorates the front of the jacket of this book. Afterwards it became apparent that this very same animal killed game hunter Baron W. von Blumenthal in 1968. The vervet or grivet *(Cercopithecus aethiops)* is a typical tree dweller, who only comes down to join a raiding party. When camping in East Africa, seal your tent-flaps securely ! In Amboseli, Keekorok and other places, these handy little devils even learned how to open a zip-fastener. Mirrors, spoons, torches, photo-lenses, shaving-brushes and tooth-brushes are all likely to have vanished when you return to your tent. Some years ago these monkeys hit the headlines when they caused Yambuku fever in Zaire and the Sudan and 800 people died. In February 1980, the virus (green monkey disease) also appeared in a Nairobi hospital.

Baboons and buffaloes

The African buffalo (*Syncerus caffer*) can weigh up 1,800 pounds (800 kilogrammes). They usually live in enormous herds of a hundred or more in Kenya and Tanzania. Old bulls often separate and live together in peace in their old age. These bulls have the heaviest horns. Apart from *homo sapiens*, with his murderous weapons, the buffalo has no enemies : even lions hesitate to attack these heavyweights. If they do, they run the risk of becoming the victims of their own recklessness. Only females and young animals, which stray from the herd, are usually attacked. Professional hunters look upon the African buffalo as one of the most dangerous animals in the continent. Even mortally wounded animals will attack. Seriously hurt, he will wait in a hidden corner to return to his attack. The hunter deserves all he gets if he wounds an animal.

During my twenty safaris I have often been in touch with baboons, especially the chackma baboon (*Papio ursinus*), also the olive baboon (*Papio anubis neumanni*) (see photos on page 147). Yet, towards the coast of the Indian Ocean, for example in Kenya, I also had enter my tent the yellow baboon (*Papio cynocephalus*), more slender, higher on its legs and lighter in colour. With their highly developed social hierarchy and their ability to adapt, and the fact that man has mastered their natural enemy the leopard, they are capable of survival if they can resist the pressure of the greatest of all primates. In any case, baboons are quite capable of defending themselves. Males, with a set of teeth equal to that of any animal of prey, would even attack a leopard and as recently as 1979 two children who were throwing stones at a group of baboons were attacked by

the leaders and killed in Ethiopia.

Mother baboons are most attentive to their young. The small infant is very vulnerable and during the first month of its life capable only of suckling and clamping itself to the mother's belly. After a month he can ride piggy-back and mother will teach him which fruits to eat and which dangers to avoid.

(Drawings by the author)

Holding on with their claws, head down, thousands of suspended straw coloured fruit bats (Eidolon helvum) wait for night before flighting. Provided with eyes ten times as sensitive as human ones and a delicate sonar system, they flutter around throughout the African night, in search of insects or fruit.

In 1966 on safari in the Budongo forest in Uganda and accompanied by the world expert in this field, John G. Williams, we discovered in our mist nets above a stream in the forest a species of bat which was entirely new to science : Glauconycteris (photo bottom left).

Honey badgers (Mellivora ratel), like the bats, are mainly active during the night. They are extremely fond of honey, and have a skin so thick that it cannot be penetrated by bees. It is one of the most courageous small animals in the wilderness and will even defend itself against a lion. In Rhodesia I saw a white game-ranger jump for his life (right onto the roof of his Land-Rover) when a honey badger, seeing its young in danger, attacked him. When a honey badger attacks, its goes straight for the genitals !

The wart hog (Phacochoerus aethiopicus) *lives in holes in the ground into which, when in danger, it retires backwards. Only its head with enormous tusks, which instil fear into any beast of prey, can then be seen. It searches for food kneeling down, moving forward to find the various grasses it likes. Root crops are no problem either, they can easily be dug up. (Photo left and centre).*

Wild boars

The giant forest hog (Hylochoerus meinterzhageni) *is a good deal larger than the wart hog. It was discovered only in 1904 by a British officer, Meinertzhagen, first in Kenya and a few years later also in the Congo region. It lives in very remote areas. I only succeeded, after weeks of searching, to film a family in the Aberdare forest. (Photos below).*

The giant euphorbia (Euphorbia candelabra) is known for its whitish latex sap which is very poisonous. The variety Euphorbia avasmontana may cause temporary or even permanent blindness when the moisture touches the eye.

The yellow-fever tree can reach a height of some 80 feet (25 metres). Explorers suffered from fever when camping beneath these giants, which grow mostly near water and are a breeding place for mosquitoes. Hence their name.

Trees

Wild figs can be found as trees, bushes or even climbers. It is certainly worthwhile hiding near one laden with ripe fruit to see what happens. Various fruit eaters, such as hornbills, turacos and monkeys come to feast on the ripe fruit.

The sausage tree (Kigelia africana) bears fruit resembling enormous sausages, up to 20 inches (50 centimetres) long and weighing several pounds. Unfortunately they are not edible. Natives make bows from this tree's very flexible branches.

The papaya tree (Carica papaya) originates from tropical America. The fruit, which is very good for the digestion, is strongly recommended to all safari enthusiasts.

The umbrella tree (Acacia tortilis) can be seen on the plains and steppes of East Africa. Giraffes adore the juicy tops and the shade is appreciated by beasts of prey as well as the author ! (see also page 73). Elephants push them over to find a tasty meal of young shoots.

The banana tree (Musa sapientum) has grown since time immemorial in India, and was introduced into Africa during the sixteenth century.

The whistling thorn (Acacia drepanolobium), a plant resembling mimosa with sharp, long thorns. The gall-nuts around the thorns are the habitat of ants (Crematogaster), which consider them an excellent home in which to raise their off-spring. The sound produced by this whistling thorn-tree comes from the wind blowing through the holes in the gall-nuts.

Plants, as well as animals, offer enormous variety in tropical Africa. Nobody who has ever seen the jacarandas or the bougainvilleas, a blaze of colour under the African sun, will be able to forget them.

In some seasons one enjoys the bright red flowers of the kaffir tree (Erythrina melanacantha) or the pale coral red of the flame tree (Erythrina abyssinica), both coral trees (photo page). Then there is the prickly pear (Opuntia vulgaris), the fruit of which can be eaten as long as one takes care of the needle-sharp thorns ! (photo top left).

The flame lily (Gloriosa superba), with its red-yellow flowers resembling orchids, can be found at the edge of the forest. The leaves which end in tendrils, attack themselves to other plants (photo centre left).

The moon-flower (Datura arborea), sometimes called angels' tears, is one of the potato family. They smell heavenly during the night but are extremely poisonous. (Photo centre right).
The flamboyant (Delonix regia) originates from Madagascar. (Photo bottom right).
Photo bottom left : Kaffir tree (Erythrina lysistemon).

The water hyacinth (Eichhornia crassipes) *floats on the water on air sacs beneath its leaves.*

The Chinese or Indian rose (Hibiscus rosa-sinensis) *originates from Asia.*

The bougainvillea, a native of South America, can be found in all tints from white to blood red.

The Tiger or spider-lily (Hymenocallis senegambica) *smells of vanilla.*

Even in the dry season in South Africa one can feel water drops when walking underneath the 'huilboer' tree.

The frangipani (Plumeria acutifolia), *which came from Mexico, flowers throughout the year.*

Orchids

Many species of orchid can be found in the tropical rain forests. They are usually epiphytes, parasitic plants which, with aerial roots, hang on to the branches. They can be admired especially at the equator in Uganda and in Natal. There are also many varieties of ground orchids.

The African monarch (Danaus chrysippus) on Kanahia laniflora. This species of butterfly contains cardenolide, a poison which makes it inedible and totally avoided by predators such as birds, lizards and monkeys.

Butterflies

Before developing into a butterfly, the African caterpillar is sometimes as beautiful and colourful as its winged successor. Some of these caterpillars, especially those of the moths, reach an enormous size by European standards.

Spiders

People who have an unwarranted fear of spiders should refrain from going for walks in the African jungle. There are species to be found which are at least ten times the size of ours. Compared to the South American species, the African spiders are generally speaking angelic. There are however a few species that give a very poisonous bite such as the baboon spider, black widow spider and banana spider. Much more dangerous are the pepper ticks which sometimes cause fevers; the fiercely biting soldier ants, though small in size, which can change naked arms or legs into hillocks of spots, and the tsetse flies which prick like a hypodermic syringe with a blunt needle. Personally I prefer the spiders, the larger the better, with their amazingly beautiful structures and splendid colourings.

Top left :
Watch out for the tiny parasitic spiders (no, they are not the spiders' young), which can be seen on the back and beside the giant spider.

Chameleons

Chameleon is the common name of one of of the most remarkable of the family of lizards. They move slowly in the bushes and their grasping feet cause a jerking movement. The tongue is very long, club-shaped and provided with a sticky secretion at its tip. It can be shot out to a remarkable distance to secure its prey, and then rapidly withdrawn. The eyes are large and independently mobile, thus enabling the creature to look simultaneously forward and backward. The colour of its skin changes in response to the environment. The fingers of a chameleon are fused into two groups, which enable it to grasp branches.

Above right :
Hoehnel's chameleon (Chamaeleo hoehnelii).

Two of the most remarkable species are the three-horned chameleon *(Chamaeleo jacksonii)*, which I only saw in the forests of Uganda, Rwanda-Burundi and eastern Zaire, and the giant chameleon *(Chamaeleo oustaleti)* which lives in the Ngong hills of Kenya. Some chameleons lay eggs, others give birth to young.

Snakes

Colobus

Facing page :
A rock python (Python sebae) *is a snake which kills its prey by constriction and can grow up to 23 feet (6.5 metres) long. Pythons feed mostly on wild fowl but sometimes also tackle small antelopes. Their excellent camouflage can be seen in the centre photograph.*
Ten poisonous cobra snakes, five of the genus Naja, live in Africa. The black forest cobra (Naja melanoleuca) *is one of them (photo bottom left). When excited they raise up the front part of their body and expand the neck. They are very poisonous but not as aggressive as other cobras. They are very fond of fish !*
One of the most lethal African snakes is the mamba (top right) (below that are snake eggs !).
The agama lizard (Agama agama), *with its bright red head and blue body, is one of the most colourful lizards in the world.*

One of the most impressive concerts I ever heard in my life was the short, four-minute chorus of the black and white fringed-faced Colobus monkeys which live on the mountain slopes and in the forests of the Aberdare and Elgon Mountains in Kenya, in the Kayonza jungle of Uganda or in the mountain forests of Meru Mountain in Tanzania.

Before daybreak suddenly all the noises made by the tree frogs, the ranas, the bats and galagos cease; to be replaced by an increasing staccato, an approaching thunder, a rattling song, by which the monkeys define their territory in voluble manner. The black and white fringed-faced monkeys or guerezas, sometimes called colobus and by ex-colonials 'magistrates' owing to their striking gown, are surely the most beautiful and most elegantly attired monkeys in the African forests. To see a troup of them, leaping from branch to branch, with their coats resembling white cloaks, skipping in the wind, is one of the most fascinating pictures one can imagine.

This warm, silk coat protects the guerezas (*Colobus polykomos* and in Swahili, *Mbega*) against the penetrating dampness and the cold nights of the forest slopes at heights, sometimes above 6,560 feet (2,000 metres). It also protects the animal against the hords of insects, tree ants and midges, which proliferate in this type of environment. Guerezas, who have the distinguishing characteristic of no thumb, feed on various types of leaves,

161

The colobus, threatened by hunters and demands of fashion, now faces another danger : yellow fever coming from the north has claimed a large number of victims from their ranks.

buds and blossoms. They seldom leave the trees, they drink rain water which they find in the cracks and holes of the tree trunks and rarely need to come down to ground level. Once in 1962, when for the first and last time I visited Tree Tops in the Aberdare Mountains, I saw six of them descending carefully from the trees. With great leaps they approached a drinking place and then rapidly disappeared.

Guerezas have snow-white young, who remain riveted to their mother's chest, whatever dizzy leaps she performs. These monkeys are master jumpers and are the greatest acrobats in the African jungle. I have seen frightened black and white colobus jump from the top of forest trees some 160 feet (50 metres) high to the lower branches of other trees – a sensational sight, with their white plumed tails and coats serving as a partial parachute. It is for their uniquely beautiful skin that these innocent and peace-loving creatures are hunted. The natives make all kinds of decorations from the skin. Head-gear, floor mats, seat covers, fire rugs – and Jomo Kenyatta himself went about waving the tail of a guereza. An identity status symbol – or just a fly-whisk ?

Despite the fact that they are a vigorously protected animal, the Ethiopian game poachers still manage to smuggle three to four thousand of these lovely monkey skins out of the country. Up to the First World War monkey fur was very popular with European ladies and the guerezas were shot on a massive scale and were practically extinguished. In 1892 alone 172,000 colobus skins appeared on the market. In 1960 26,529 colobus skins were sold. But whereas in Zaire – neither legally nor illegally – the white-tailed guereza is not hunted, it does occur elsewhere in East Africa.

According to the Congolese, the death throes and lamentations of a dying colobus strongly resemble those of men. However, the members of the Wandorobo tribe in Kenya are so fond of the meat of the fringed-faced monkeys, that they take the disturbing noise in their stride. They exchange the skins with their neighbours the Masai, who make the hair into leg decorations which hang down their calves. Fashion has always been the greatest enemy and source of disaster to many animals. One has only to think of the great white egret, the bird of paradise and the leopard.

The most beautiful black and white colobus I ever saw were in the Aberdare Mountains where I often camped with Gordon Harvey. They are also

The misty slopes of Mount Kenya, 17,040 feet (5,194 metres) high and, despite its location on the equator, eternally capped in snow. This is the favourite haunt of the fringe-faced monkeys.

163

found in the forest of Mount Elgon (14,178 feet / 4,320 metres), where they are very tame, but they were most numerous in the Ruwenzori Massif near Fort Portal in Uganda. In the Budongo primeval forest and along the banks of the Nile we saw, in the land which at that time had not yet been ravaged by Field-Marshal Amin Dada, troups ot ten to twenty of these beautiful creatures.

The photograph you see here was made in the Bwamba forest in the Semliki valley in Uganda, where I could approach within 65 feet (20 metres) of a family.

The high mountain road right through the Impenetrable Forest in south-west Kigezi offered a marvellous opportunity for studying the guerezas. The narrow strip hacked out of the rock walls is, in some places, at the same level as the upper regions of the Hagenia forest. Late at night, this presents the opportunity for an eye-to-eye encounter with the feeding colobus monkeys. As their diet mainly consists of *Rauwolfia* and *Podocarpus gracillior* a close watch should be kept on specimens of those trees.

Experts know that these monkeys, like nearly all monkeys, are inquisitive and can be tempted to come close by. It is sufficient just to imitate the true sign of a copious meal; a loud belch, and the response is quick ! We have repeated this experiment (on an empty stomach) on many occasions and can vouch for its effectiveness.

Meru

The region where, after Baringo and Tsavo (above the Galana River), I have camped most, is without doubt the immense Meru Reserve, north-east of Mount Kenya. Its fantastic diversity of plants and animals; and the fact that it is tucked far away from the tourist areas, in an unviolated part of Africa, has always appealed to me. For weeks on end I did not see a soul. I camped there close to the equator (see map). There abounded lions, leopards, and cheetahs; hippos in the Rojewero and Tana Rivers; Grevy and Burchell's zebras; Grant's gazelles, lesser kudu and gerenuk. Now-here in Africa did I see larger herds of buffalo than here. In November 1977 I was fortunate enough to see an enormous herd of over one thousand. But, after all, it is the only place where the white, as well as the black, rhinoceros can still be found.

One of my favourite camping sites is in the Meru region, near the equator in North-east Kenya. We often set up camp here under the shade of the enormous umbrella trees on the banks of the Rojewero river. There was an abundance of animals : white and black rhinos, elephants, giraffes, gnus, oryx, elands and leopards, not to mention an enormous variety of birds. Leave a finger's depth of water in your washing bowl near the night storm-lamp and an hour later you will have a mosaic of numerous insects, among them multi-coloured beetles, moths and mosquitoes.
Below left : The Tana river.

For the ornithologist, Meru is a real joy, equal to the highly praised Tsavo region. Years ago, a part of what used to be a wild reserve, now a national park, had a 'wilderness area'. This was an area without roads, where you could camp accompanied by armed 'rangers' and be followed by porters with food and equipment. Unfortunately, this is now forbidden, and there are even parts of this unique park which are closed altogether. With sadness I think of the days when I could approach elephants and rhinos on foot. There is so much difference between photographing from a metal box on wheels where one feels like a prisoner, unlike the animal which can roam about freely. Now it is man who is behind bars !

From just under 3,300 feet (1,000 metres) high at the Nyambeni mountains at its most northern border, the Meru National Park slopes down to less than 100 metres (330 feet) at the mighty Tana River, its boundary in the south-east sector. The most important rivers in this paradise are the Rojewero, the Ura, the Kiolu and the aforementioned Tana River. All these rivers are overhung by the doum palm of Egypt *(Hyphaene coriacea)*, wild dates *(Phoenix reclinata)*, and the raffia palms *(Raphia rufia)*; but this paradise has many other plants besides, *Combretum* bush in the northern sector, *Commiphera* in the south. In between there are marsh grasses and acacia woods and in the far north even an offshoot of the Ngaia forest, with enormous fig trees, covered with lianas in which one expects every moment to see Tarzan appear.

The south-eastern boundary is formed by the mighty hippo-occupied Tana River and the wildly foaming Adamson's Falls.

(See photo on next page).

The coconut palm (Cocos nucifera) was imported from Indonesia before the birth of Christ. They can be found along the entire coast of Kenya and Tanzania. They are an important source of food and oil, and the leaves are used to cover roofs or for weaving mats or partitions. The fibres can be used to make excellent rope. Coconut milk is not drunk by some natives as they believe it makes them sterile. The palm trees are 'tapped' for pombe or mnazi which is Swahili for palm wine. Very intoxicating !

Bixa orellana is found along the ocean coast. The red flowers provide a pigment which is used for the colouring of the shuka of the Masai. The natives rub their skin with it, to protect themselves against insects.

In Kenya one hardly speaks of the Indian Ocean, but rather of the Coral Coast; and not without reason. Enormous structures were built over the ages by colonies of these marine creatures.

The Indian Ocean

The most common tribe along the Kenya coast is the Giriama. They are small in stature, and although they are Islamic, or converted to Christianity after the appearance of the first missionaries in 1844, their belief in all forms of witchcraft and magic remains.

The Kenya and Tanzania coast of the Indian Ocean stretches for 830 miles (1,330 kilometres) from Lumu in Kenya down to Mtwara in Tanzania. Although that coast is normally exceedingly hot it becomes cooler in the south east monsoon winds which blow continuously from April to October. This is the time to sail to the Persian Gulf and India. The dhows, sea-worthy ships usually owned by Arabian merchants, sail for Mombasa, Zanzibar and Dar-es-Salaam. From November to March when the wind blows from the north east and is called 'Kaskazi'. Since the middle ages the coast of Kenya has been visited by merchants from western Europe and Arabia searching for slaves and ivory.

Whether they are Giriama women from along the coast of the Indian Ocean or any other tribe, they carry everything on the head. Contrary to the west European, they know how to use their heads ! I have seen everything transported on women's heads, from stone jars with 35 pints (20 litres) of water (see photo on page 201) to milk bottles, sewing machines and stamps (admittedly, they had a stone on them to hold them down).

The Jamia mosque in the capital of Kenya, Nairobi, indicates the Indian presence in East Africa. In 1896 the British colonists imported 32,000 as cheap labour from India in order to build the railway lines from Mombasa to Uganda. When the railway was finished in 1901, quite a number of Indians remained and sent for their relatives. As it was forbidden, by the colonial government, for them to cultivate the land, they specialised in trade and can now be found in the furthest corners of East Africa. When independence was granted in 1963, there were over 139,000 Asians in Kenya.

Southern Africa

Africa on stilts ! A young Tswana in Botswana shows how it should be done. As he grows older this young bushman will find life more serious.

The young Botswana dweller walks on stilts in order to appear taller. This is also the aim of the Zulu rickshaw-runner, with his enormous, very colourful headgear in Durban, the favourite resort and holiday place of the South Africans. This headgear is now becoming traditional custom.

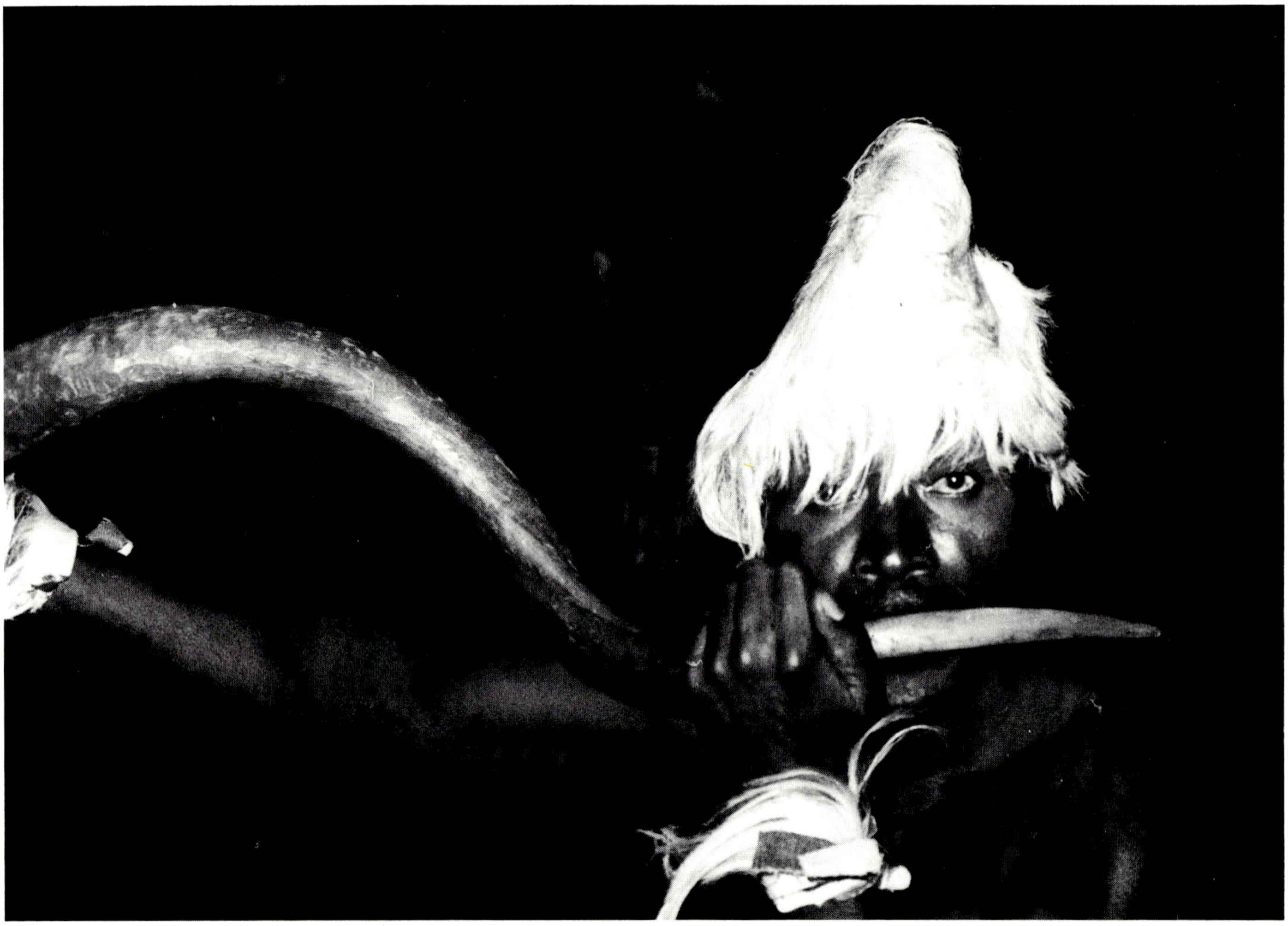

Music and dance play an important part in ritual ceremonies. Here a Zulu in South Africa blows an invitation to a dance on his kudu horn. Around the turn of the century the Herero tribe, which was threatened with extinction in Namibia, crossed the Kalahari desert. The survivors reached the Okavango region and settled down. As they were wholly without property, they offered themselves as labour. Gradually they worked their way up to what they were in their own country : farmers and owners of large herds of cattle. Things changed. They are now the wealthiest employers of the Okavango delta in Botswana.

Photos on next page : The Kariba Dam and the Zambesi have the best known predatory fish, the tiger fish (Hydrocinus lineatus) (top left). Like the piranhas they hunt in shoals and are equally bloodthirsty. Right : Matusadona, a forgotten paradise by Lake Kariba. Below : between 1956 and 1961 the mighty Zambesi river was conquered in the Rhodesia of those days, now Zimbabwe. A gigantic retaining dam was built which flooded more than 25,000 square miles (4,000 square kilometres) and formed Lake Kariba. Thousands of animals were killed. Only the tops of trees still point their accusing fingers above the water surface as silent witnesses.

It needs little imagination to realise the emotion David Livingstone, the well-known missionary and explorer, must have felt when he was the first white man to see the Victoria Falls in 1855. The largest river of south-east Africa plunges here, across a width of 6,000 feet (1,808 metres), from a height of 390 feet (119 metres). Dr Livingstone gave the greatest waterfalls of the whole of Africa the name of his queen, Queen Victoria of Britain, but the Makololom, the tribe of the region, still call them Mosi-oa-tunga or 'the smoke which thunders'. Around the middle of April, when the summer rains swell the Zambesi River 1,400 miles long (2,260 kilometres), 240 million cubic gallons (345 million cubic litres) plunge through eight ravines. It is one of the most spectacular views one can imagine. The 'water smoke' can be seen at a distance of some 60 miles (100 kilometres) and it is understandable that the nearby vegetation profits from this continuous spray.

One of the most remarkable flowers in this constantly humid jungle section at the Victoria Falls is the African tulip (Haemanthus multiflorus martijn). Also called blood lily, powderpuff Lily, fireball lily or pin cushion. These beautiful African 6-8 inch (15-20 centimetre) red flower balls grow from a large bulb.

The Masai

The once much feared Masai, the lionmen, who at one time terrorised almost the whole of East Africa with raids on their neighbours, are only a shadow of the past, a picturesque anachronism. The Masai believe, Lengai (their god) created the earth with fertile meadows – grass for the cows of the Masai. Things could not be simpler. According to the Masai, it would be an insult to their god if they ploughed or worked on the earth.

Around AD 1700 the vanguard of the Nilo-Hamites, the Masai, reached a region which they named Nairobi, or 'place of the cold water'. When the Europeans appeared towards the end of the nineteenth century, they found the Masai had already spread out to what is now northern Tanzania. The Masai called the white man *L'Ojoejoe* or 'hairy one', and since he did not possess any cattle, he was shunned, as was everything possessed by him. In 1869, the Samburu infected them with cholera and, immediately before the white man appeared with all his power around 1880, they were afflicted with smallpox.

At the the turn of the century, their cattle were struck by the dangerous runderpest (a lung disease blown over from Asia) and they themselves faced extinction.

The Masai girls and women wear heavy, multi-coloured necklaces and bracelets, ear-rings of copper wire and similar rings around their ankles. No one in Africa is as extensively decorated as the Masai beauties. As these attributes are very popular with tourists, the women sometimes sell them. Some Masai women make such beaded ornaments specifically for sale to the tourists. After all, history repeats itself. The white man brought the shells and worthless shiny stones into the country as currency. Now the African is selling them back to him.

A Masai – a real one – lives almost entirely on the milk, blood and meat of his cattle. They are real blood drinkers. By shooting a specially cut arrow-head into the neck artery of a cow, the blood can be caught in a calabash. Afterwards the small wound is sealed with fresh dung. The tourniquet which tied the artery is loosened and the beast is left in peace for some weeks.

Children have the right to drink the pure blood. Adults drink the blood mixed with milk. It is their main diet. They do not eat farinaceous food, fish or vegetables. It is the blood of his cattle which keeps the Masai fit, not the meat. Their exclusive diet of blood and milk, which not only contains protein but also fats and carbohydrates, makes them one of the healthiest tribes in Africa. Western physicians have studied their exclusive milk-and-blood diet and say that heart disease is unknown among the Masai. A unique built-in mechanism protects them against a high cholesterol level.

Cattle are a status symbol of the Masai, but it is the quantity, not the quality, that is important. The cows (more than one million for the 155,000 Masai in Kenya and 80,000 in Tanzania) are economically worthless (for the country).

Only the Morans or warriors are entitled to have hair. All the others including women and girls have their heads shaven. The hair of the Moran is rubbed with red ochre and grease and cleverly plaited.

Young male Masai are trained to become warriors and live together in age-groups or clans. In former times, the Moran showed his courage by killing a lion with his spear or by catching him by the tail. This is now forbidden under Pax brittannica and uhuru (or freedom). The Masai is now only concerned with his status symbol : his cattle. The more cows he possesses, the richer he thinks he is. To keep a lion away from his cows, he now uses a 'soup spoon of coopertox' (a product used by the veterinary surgeon in which the cows are dipped to free them from ticks). He plants it in a carcass and that means the end of the lion. Poisoned ! After having spent seven or eight years as a Moran warrior, the men are shaved, marry and take up their place amongst the elders. From then onwards their life is peaceful as the women do the work and the cattle provide them with all their needs : blood, milk and meat. Masai do not eat game meat.

Samburu-morans with ilmasi wala headdress, a kind of overhanging fringe which prevents the sun from shining in their eyes, just as we wear a cap. Samburu means butterfly. Like real butterflies they flutter from one grazing field to the next. Most Samburu decorations and habits, including circumcision, are the same as those of the Masai.

Marriageable Masai girl from the Kedong valley. When a Masai girl is sought in marriage the suitor offers a gift of cows. The price varies between twenty to one hundred head of cattle. The daughter of a chieftain cannot be had for anything less than 150 cows. The social status of the girl is of great importance.

Although closely related to the Masai, the decoration of the Samburu women differs from that of the Masai. From early youth they pile up neck-rings which become more and more impressive as the years go by. By European standards it would be a considerable burden to walk with this load under the tropical sun. But who can argue with fashion?

In north Kenya, near the border of Ethiopia, live the Borana, biblical descendants of the son of Ham : easily recognisable from their fine features and elegant build which clearly reveals their Ethiopian origin (see also photograph bottom right on page 185). They talk Galla, a dialect which is also spoken in Ethiopia. The Borana are shepherds like the Nilo-Hamites.

Masai cattle on their way to a water hole. Enormous quantities of emaciated cows, which, tightly packed together, trot the same paths for years on end, pull out the grass by the roots, and cause inevitable erosion. The Samburu, as well as the Turkana and the Masai, possess cattle in excess of adequate pastures.

In the nort-east of Kenya, near the border with Somalia, the camel (or dromedary) replaces the cow. It is one of the most useful domestic animals which man has tamed but at the same time the most prone to biting and obstinacy. It is called 'the ship of the desert' as under certain circumstances this animal can go up to fourteen days without water. The Korokoro confirmed this, adding that the animal will have gulped down some 26 pints (50 litres) of water before setting this record. A camel can drink over 175 pints (100 litres) of water in less than ten minutes.

An elder of the Borana, a Hamatite tribe which we found around Marsabit.

Besides the camels which drank at the Tana river, there were also numerous goats quenching their thirst. Goats are certainly the oldest domestic animals. A goat is a tough beast which multiplies rapidly and eats what other animals refuse, they have an all-destroying influence on the vegetation, they eat everything within reach, even the seedlings of young trees, thus making it impossible for nature to recover itself. The ownership of their goats causes the natives a great deal of worry. One may have 176 and another 68 and they try to keep them apart when they meet at the watering place. Quarrelling and fighting are a normal occurrence on such occasions.

Water is of vital importance. Women, who must fetch the water for household consumption, have to walk as much as 6 miles (10 kilometres) each day to get it.

The Turkana, as the Samburu and the Masai, are of Nilo-Hamitic origin. They are courageous warriors who drove the Masai from their lands around the 1850s and were the last tribe to be conquered by the British. The decoration which is placed below the mouth in the chin is remarkable. It used to be made of ivory, but now aluminium is used. Although many old habits are disgarded, some warriors still wear the mouth shield, which goes through the nostrils and prevents evil spirits entering one of the nine holy openings.

Contrary to the neighbouring tribes, the Turkana do not practise circumcision. They are constantly in trouble with the tribes in the north which involves them in raids and quarrels. They always carry two spears.

The enormous neck-rings worn by the Samburu, Pokot, Rendille and Turkana women are made of doum palm fibre.

189

The Turkanas living along the west bank of Lake Turkana sometimes attempt to fish. They use a kind of trap for the purpose. The fish is usually dried in the sun and can then be kept. The Turkana woman (photo centre) is in mourning, which can be seen by her forehead which is covered with grey ash.

A fisherman shows us a tilapia he has caught. This is the most common fish found in the enormous lake. Lake Turkana is a true birds' paradise. Flamingoes, pelicans, cormorants and a great variety of migrant birds can be seen here.

Lake Turkana

Lake Turkana, sometimes called the Jade Sea, is 250 miles long (400 kilometres) and nearly 40 miles wide (60 kilometres). There are plenty of fish and Nile perch (*Lates albertianus*) the largest freshwater fish in Africa, measuring 6 feet (2 metres) and weighing up to 330 pounds (150 kilogrammes). It is remarkable that this lake with its blue-green colouring has no outlet although several rivers flow into it. Due to evaporation, the lake, of 1,900 square miles (3,000 square kilometres), sometimes drops approximately 10 feet (3 metres) in level.

In the middle of the enormous Lake Turkana (formerly Lake Rudolf) is Central Island, a small group of uninhabitable extinct volcanoes. It is a frightening volcanic place, which conveys the sensation that this is the end of the world. After a difficult climb with the volcanic ash slipping away beneath one's feet, one reaches the upper rims of the water-filled craters.

These three lakes each have a different colour; brown, green and blue. As this phenomenon remains constant under all weather conditions, the reason must be found in the varying depths and soil substrata which foster growth of different algae.

The inner lakes and the surroundings of Central Island are alive with crocodiles. The quality of the water makes the skin of the crocodile unsuitable for trade – I once swam in it; it is very alkaline and thus the wet stones and rocks are extremely slippery. Unsuitable because round hard discs – 'buttons' develope in the skin which is then no use commercially.

Flamingoes and pelicans gather peacefully together along the banks of Lake Turkana.
Living exclusively on fish, the gregarious pelicans are doing very well here. On land they appear rather plump, but once airborne they become very elegant owing to their streamlined frame and mighty wings.

Virunga

Virunga with its lovely sounding name, is a volcanic mountain range north-west of Lake Kivu in Zaire at the border of Uganda, near Rwanda. Here lies the Virunga National Park which is 185 miles long (300 kilometres) and 25 miles wide (40 kilometres), seen against a back-cloth of the Mitumba mountain range of some 5,000 square miles (8,000 square kilometres). The Park used to be called Albert Park. The range encompasses the Semliki, the Rutshuru, the Via Sacra, the Rwindi plain and the unique Ufumbiro mountains. A paradise which, it is to be hoped, will remain free from interference (see bottom page 195).

At the edges of this beautiful country, the deforestation (bottom left) is constantly increasing, as a result of the population explosion. On the equator this has some far-reaching effects. The evaporation here is three times as great as in Europe, which is why, in the tropics, any shade of tree or bush is of vital importance.

Top right : a member of the Batutsi tribe in Rwanda, known for their aristocratic features, their elegant body structure and their dancing.

Ishango, a name to remember because time stood still here. This is how Africa must have been one hundred years ago.

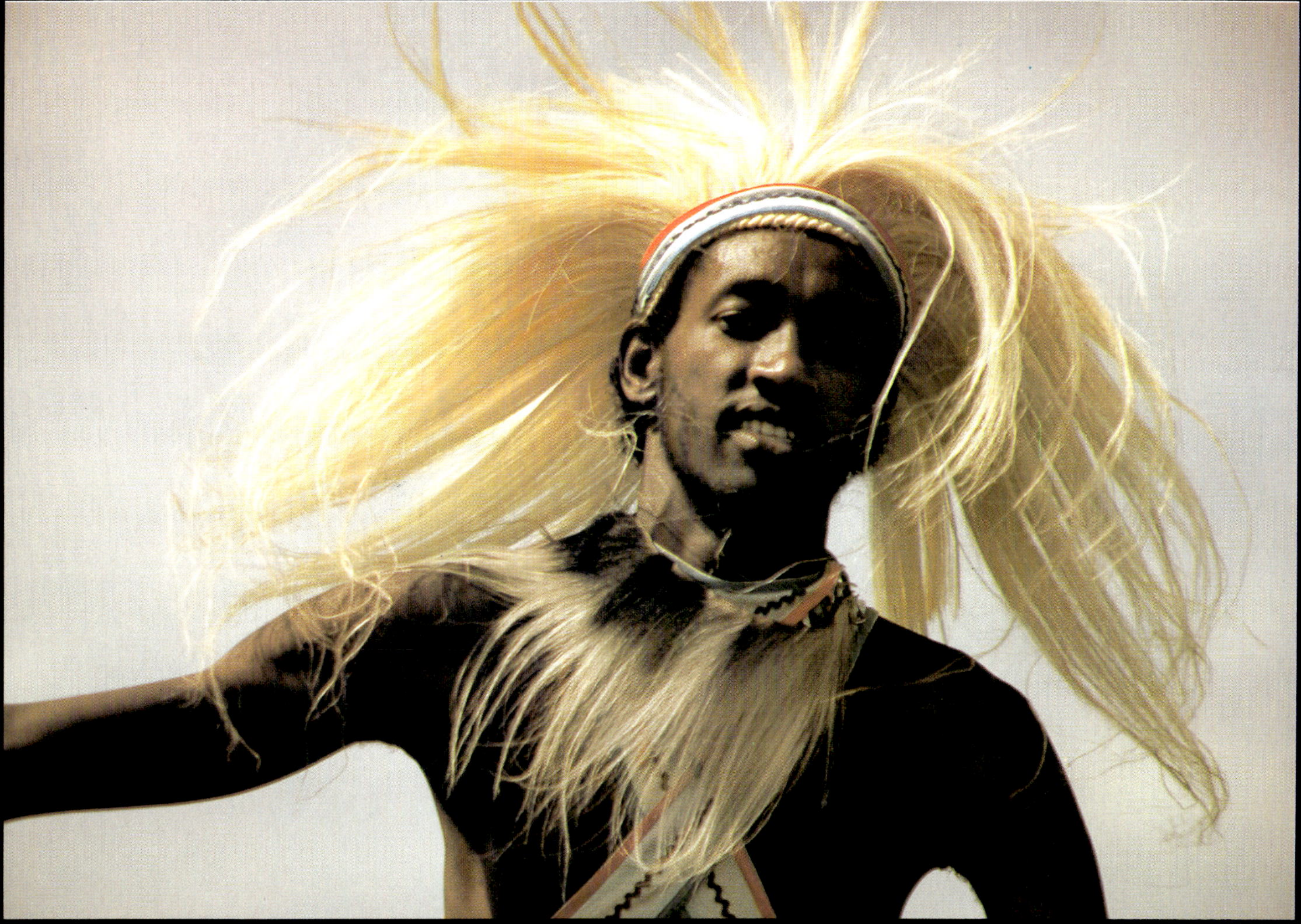

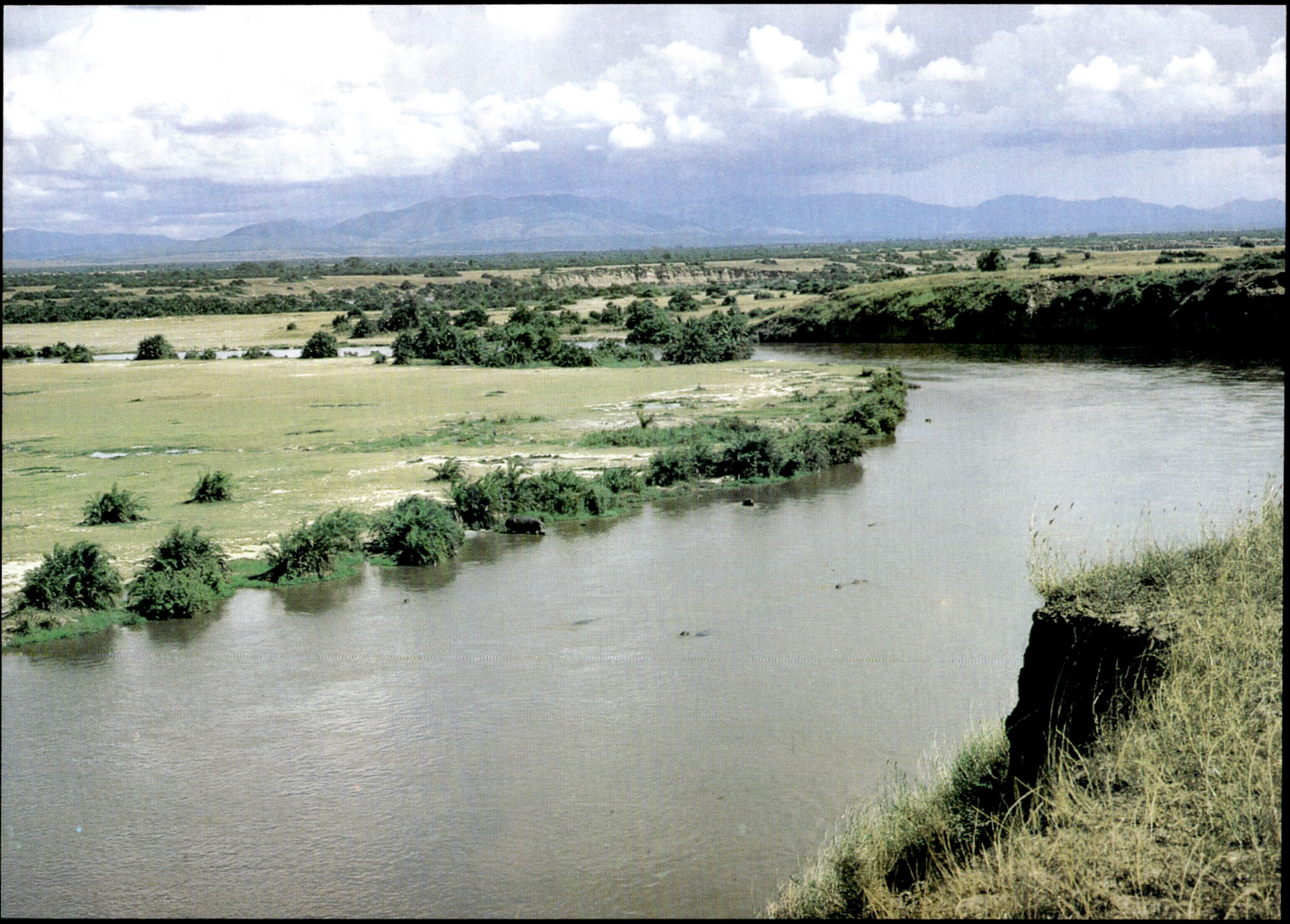

Ishango with the impressive Semliki River at our feet – the place in Africa where I would like to be buried. However, it owes its name to a misunderstanding. Semliki means in the local language 'I do not know'. It was the reply given by a native to one of the white explorers when he asked the name of the river.

The former Lake Edward, which for eight long years carried the name Lake Idi Amin, is now waiting under the sun for a new name. It is full of fish and the native population was granted permission to build a fishing village in the middle of the National Park, Vitshumbi. Daily the miraculous draught of fishes is repeated here to the great joy of the numerous pelicans which are quick to gulp down the fish waste. A gorgeous meal !(Bottom page 197).

Buffaloes and topi-antelopes in the Rwindi Reservation. Fewer than fifty years ago the animal population here was truly remarkable.

The banana is a frequently grown fruit in Africa and has a high food potential. Some varieties are large and yellow, others small, reddish and fat. The green banana is boiled or steamed. Everybody knows the banana, but its flower is less familiar (photo below).

East of the road from Rutshuru to Goma one can see, in the distance, the Nyarogongo 1,200 feet (3,470 metres) and with a crater of 1,100 yards diametre (1 kilometre). A continuous cloud of smoke rises from the enormous cauldron of boiling, red-hot lava, in this largest active volcano in the world. Between 1938 and 1950 and again from 1967 to 1971 a series of eruptions succeeded one another. The road between Goma and Bukavu was flooded with lava and a number of villages were wiped from the face of the earth.

It is hoped that the Virunga National Park, established in 1925 by Albert, King of the Belgians, will remain what it is : a natural sanctuary, one of the most perfect on earth. There are 26,000 hippos (census by J.P. von der Becke in 1975), the largest concentration in Africa. With its mountain gorillas, its elephants, antelopes and lions, its plains, forests and volcanoes, fauna and flora, it is a microcosm of all Africa.

The Cameroons

West Africa, where I studied the Cameroons and the Upper Volta, forms a great contrast to East Africa. At the border of Nigeria there is the Mandara mountain range, which has a special structure caused by erosion and other geological phenomena throughout the ages. The volcanic monoliths of Kapsiki reach heights of more than 330 feet (100 metres) and give the impression of being on another planet.

At the beginning of the last century the inhabitants, the Matakam, were chased from their fertile plains by the invading Fulbees. They settled in the inhospitable Mandara mountains. The occupiers, all Mussulmen, named the primitive mountain dwellers Kirdis, a name they still keep and which means 'heathen'.

Time has stopped in the Mandara mountains and some tribes, the Kirdis, Podokwos and Mofus, live still as they did in the middle ages. The roots of age-old trees give some protection against the scorching heat and the women, true to the centuries-old traditions, continue to tattoo themselves.

A young woman, whom I sketched, asked afterwards for my pencil and not the drawing. Expecting artistic talent I presented it to her, but it was immediately promoted to decorate the ear.

A row of primitive huts, built of stones and clay, belonging to the Mafus in the hamlet of Saree in the North Cameroons.

The Bobo-niénégue are animists, for them the soul is the primary cause of any life-phenomenon.

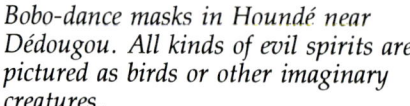

Bobo-dance masks in Houndé near Dédougou. All kinds of evil spirits are pictured as birds or other imaginary creatures.

Sabu-girl from the surrounding area of Bobo-Dioulasso. Keeping their balance provides the African beauties with their elegant walk. A tip for European ladies if they wish to parade equally majestically : walk some distance daily with about thirty-five pints of water on your head.

As in the Cameroons, the tribes living in the fertile plains were chased by invaders into the mountains. The Toros, sometimes called troglodites, built homes for themselves in the rocks.

Upper Volta

Admittedly, I saw much folklore in the Upper Volta and the artistic appeal was much greater than in East Africa, but as for the fauna, I was very disappointed. West Africa was 'civilised' several centuries before East Africa. Civilisation – as we know from experience – has disastrous consequences for the fauna. The African population is ever increasing. The precise situation in the Upper Volta is not known to me, but in Kenya there is an annual population increase of some 3.5 per cent – the highest in the world! The flight to the cities causes difficulties in the food supply and also the livestock need to increase rapidly. The food problem has become more and more acute for the African. Primitive shepherds prevent the animals from roaming, they prefer quiet, devoted animals. Sheep are excellent for the purpose.

Uganda

In Uganda, once the home of the elephants, these giants can now only survive on small islands amidst an ocean of people. Only a few backs remain for the Pia piac birds. More than 90 per cent of the elephants have vanished from Uganda during the last decade.

I consider Uganda one of the most beautiful countries of all Africa. In its 91,000 square miles (with 13,000 of them water) there are the most impressive lakes, the Mountains of the Moon, rolling fields, impenetrable forest and foaming waterfalls. There is an impressive variety of animal species plus the mighty Nile. Irrespective of the devastating influence of recent leaders, I consider the population to be the most friendly and lovable of all Africa.

The Murchison Falls in north-west Uganda, renamed Kabalega by Amin Dada after the National Park, in which they are situated. Here the entire Nile rushes through open gorges, some narrow enough to be jumped by an Olympic athlete, only to thunder down some 165 feet (50 metres) lower, dragging along masses of fish, which are eagerly awaited by one of the largest concentrations of crocodiles on earth.

The ivory of the Ugandan and Zairan elephant is much thinner than that of the Kenyan elephant. This is no deterrent to the poachers. According to a census which was carried out by scientists in the Kabalega National Park, fewer than 1,000 elephants remain alive from a herd which numbered some 14,000.

There has been some talk of shooting a large proportion of the hippopotamus population in order to can it for feeding the hungry population.

Lake Victoria, discovered by Speke and Grant in 1858, covers 43,000 square miles (69,485 square kilometres) and is the largest but one freshwater lake in the world. It could hold Holland and Belgium put together. It is 260 feet deep (80 metres) and is the main water source of the Nile. Along its banks are the three East African States, Kenya, Uganda and Tanzania. The high waterlines have for centuries left contrasting stripes on the rocks of the superb islands which are spread like pearls along the banks : Rubondo, Irugwa, Bugala, Nabuyongo, Sohi, Nkose (sanctuary of the Sitatunga), Ssese, Fumve, Sanaana.

One of the most remarkable tribes which I met in East Africa was the Karamojong. They live in the dry savannahs of North-East Uganda. I think they are closely related to the Turkana and Pokot of Kenya, from whom they are only separated by a mountain range.

Unlike the Masai, the other Nilo-Hamites, the women of the Karamojong wear iron neck-rings instead of beads, small shells and other shiny objects. The men are totally naked (see next page).

The huts of the Karamojong are examples of mat plaiting.

A Karamojong has always a small hand-carved wooden seat handy. If it is time to sleep, then it will support his neck in order to protect the impressive hairstyle.

In Uganda it was common to see pipe-smoking women (see also page 204), but whether or not this had something to do with emancipation I shall never know. The fact that loads are carried on the head and children on the back is traditional for the whole of Africa.

Next page :
The extremely dry, hot and barren Karamoja region in north-east Uganda with its towering termite mounds (bottom left) consisting of earth and the semi-digested cellulose of the blind, soft-skinned termites (which are devoured by the natives as delicacies when they emerge after the first heavy rains as 'flying ants') and form a stark contrast to the much higher fertile, carefully cultivated uplands of the south-west Kigezi (top left).

The Karuma rapids of the Nile in the Kabalega region (top right).

The Kidego National Park, at the border with the Sudan (bottom right).

The tropical impenetrable rain forest is a world on its own, with rich vegetation, where the light can hardly penetrate.

The fat-bellied borassus palm (Borassus aethiopum) is eminently suitable for making canoes, – small boats. Elephants adore the large orange fruits which taste like over-ripe mangoes.

Ahmed

16 February 1973; at least 186 miles (more than 300 kilometres) separated us from civilisation. In the morning we had left Isiolo, the last settlement and the true begining of the Northern Frontier. Along the Matthews Range we had passed through the sweltering hot and endless barren Kaisut desert. The Land-Rover was full up – overloaded really – our destination, Marsabit. Behind the wheel was Peter Kanyari, Kikuyu. In the back, pressed in amidst a ton of camping and filming equipment, and food for several weeks, always with a grin on his face, was minuscule Ntiso our cook, general factotum and *kipsigi*. On his lap were twenty-four eggs, wrapped in cardboard, fresh from Isiolo, which he would protect with his life. I wondered if they would remain unbroken in the unbearable heat with the endless jogging of the heavy vehicle on the extremely poor road. There were no motorways in those days to Ethiopia, simply tracks of the most primitive kind.

I am always full of wonder when after a full day's journey through the extremely desolate sandy desert, the road suddenly climbs to above 6,560 feet (2,000 metres) and reaches a lush green area. Above on the high plateau awaits the leafy forest, with vivid blue lakes, the Gof craters; Sokorte Dika - Gof Bongoli - Lake Paradise. In an old book written by Martin Johnston, I had read that after a long hard trek, he had found this crater lake and given it the name Lake Paradise. It had been my dream for a long time to admire this wonder of nature. My youthful romanticism was not disappointed. *This was* Paradise. Hurriedly, my two black friends made camp. I had selected an open space at the edge of the forest, with a view over the lake, underneath an age-old tree covered in Old Man's Beard. Within a quarter of an hour my 'house' was ready for occupation. A tent is a useful thing, although you can hardly stand erect in it, but, after all, it is only intended for horizontal occupation during the night. The total weight is 5 1/2 pounds (2.5 kilogrammes), complete with ground sheet, and it is easily transportable. Jeffie Kent, whose parents, John and Valerie Kent organised my first safari in 1962, and whom I knew when in south Kinangop, when Jeffie was only sixteen, willingly gave me such a tent as a present.

My small tent at Lake Paradise, on the edge of the forest.

Peter, asked permission to drive to Marsabit in order to buy 'petroli' for the coming days. Of course Ntiso had to go with him, to help, so to speak. Earlier, when passing through the only street Marsabit possessed at that time, we had spotted a pump station, a *duka* (trading shop for everything under the sun, with the usual Indian in charge) and a bar. The fact that my helpers wanted to buy petrol, I did not doubt, but it occurred to me that the noisy and over-crowded pub was a greater attraction. Yet, I did not mind seeing the vehicle vanish between the majestic trees. On the contrary, I felt rather glad. At last, I was quite alone in the primeval forest – blissful solitude. Before it became dark, they would be back, with or without a fresh chicken. And Ntiso, the cook, would make something tasty then. During earlier camping days in the high Nguruman mountains, on the borders of Tanzania, he had shown his worth and knew my favourites, soup and fruit.

Lake Paradise, one of the crater lakes on Mount Marsabit.

The next morning before five o'clock, and before the sun had risen, I would wake them. Peter had no easy life with me. My *semama* (stop), *hapa* (here), *angalia* (careful), and *kwenda* (go on) were heard all the time. I was there to work and not to play and Peter was well aware of that. But now my two helpers could leave me alone for a couple of hours. Their small tent was hardly visible a little distance away. I was resting in my folding chair in front of my tent, legs stretched out in front of me, field-glasses dangling on my chest, and my Tusker beer next to me, blissfully happy, enjoying the last reflections on the little lake. There was no wind and beyond the barking of a frightened baboon, and the monotonous humming of the cicadas, it was remarkably quiet. The sun had now set with a blood-red halo behind the tops of the forest trees. It would be dark within twenty minutes. I was enjoying it all intensely. The temperature dropped, the oppressive heat vanished and glorious scents wafted from the surrounding forest. On the other side, where my explorations would take me the following day, I had detected a tree overgrown by golden-yellow orchids. Soon, when Peter and the cook came back, the quiet peace would be broken. Peter would light an enormous wood fire, our camp-fire, from the branches he had collected with Ntiso in the forest. Of course, I could do it myself, but I preferred to remain where I was, watching the ever-repeating miracle of day turning into night and the contrasting silhouettes of the decorative forest trees and listening to the last call of a turaco.

Suddenly immediately to my right at a distance of less than 32 feet (10 metres) slowly, without a sound and wholly ignoring me, an elephant appeared. Without turning my head, I could see him from the corner of my eye … and more were coming … at least ten of them. They marched forward, one behind another, straight for the lake. They moved in their characteristic elastic, soundless manner, as if walking on rubber-soled shoes; enormous beasts in the falling darkness; soft imposing shadows. In setting up the camp I had spotted the fresh droppings of buffaloes and elephants, but had not thought that this very spot was on their route to their favourite pub. With increasing amazement, from my front row seat I could see them frolicking in the swamp. The enormous grey colossi filled me with great respect. Although not frightened, I dared not move. I know no animal which radiates such peace and majesty. Yet, I wondered what would happen if the huge animals, which had now spread out around me in a half circle, suddenly panicked. I knew so many people who had been killed by elephants. (The elephant on the cover of the book was photographed by the author just one day before he killed Baron von Blumenthal on 17th January 1968, in Momella, near Arusha, Tanzania.) My little tent was no protection at all and the nearest tree was further away than the nearest elephant. Then the buffaloes arrived. It was nearly fully dark now as, with their heads bent down low under the burden of their enormous horns, they, too, passed on my right. Their soundless passing turned into a sludgy plodding of hooves in the mud when they reached the edge of the water. There were far more noises, when buffaloes and elephants met at the waterhole, snorting, sniffing, protesting and low grumbles. It was practically quite dark now. The buffaloes had gone deeper into the water, they love mud baths.

Suddenly, all became very still, I could just see the elephants raise their trunks, carefully feel the air. Then with much stamping and splashing, they went away.

I wondered what had happened when suddenly to my left, I saw three new arrivals, who had caused the herd to vanish. In the remaining light I could distinguish the enormous tusks of the colossus who had now appeared on the scene. Carefully I raised my field-glasses to my eyes. Even in the dark, the refined German technical instrument proved its worth. I shook : this was Ahmed ! The king of the elephants ! For him I had made the journey to Marsabit. He was the legendary, most protected animal in Africa : the elephant with the greatest, mightiest ivory in Africa. Each tusk weighed some 200 pounds (90 kilogrammes) and he had two … more than twice my weight on his head. He, himself, standing more than 10 feet (3 metres) high, weighed some 6 tons.

In November of the previous year President Jomo Kenyatta had taken this animal under his personal protection by issuing a decree granting the majestic elephant complete protection, with the order not to kill or worry him.

Peter Jenkins had shown me photographs, taken at the time, of the giant, and Bill Woodley, years ago, had made me envy him, when, during his time as chief park warden of Marsabit, he had taken various shots. Only now, after the end of the Shifta skirmishes (Somali gangs who made the entire Northern Frontier unsafe between 1964 and 1968) and the construction of the so-called motorway, direct to Ethiopia, was there an opportunity to visit Ahmed. John Alexander had already offered me hospitality in his luxurious tent camp so that I could admire Ahmed at ease. However, I had refused. Tourist camps are usually rather noisy establishments, with electric pumps, engines and whisky-talk.

It was for Ahmed that I'd come to Marsabit and now on the first evening I saw him ! However, the darkness was nearly complete. The enormous ivory of the giant gleamed in the soft shadow. Reflected in the water, his tusks appeared to be dripping, shining and bent towards each other … and even more colossal.

For a single moment I considered withdrawing quietly into my little tent to switch on the flash on my camera. But I remained and watched. What on earth would happen if I sneaked towards Ahmed and suddenly created a blinding light ? What would be the reaction of the two askaris, the two younger elephants who always accompanied Ahmed ? I thought of Aruba when during a February night, lying with Gordon and Joe Cheffings in a flat boat sliding towards drinking elephants, I used my flash and blinded them. The consequences could be far more dangerous now. After all, I could film the patriarch Ahmed tomorrow, or the day after; at least – so I thought.

I heard the dull rumbling in the stomachs of the dark giant shadows. I saw the huge ears flap quietly to and fro. I felt endlessly small and minute – tolerated as an insignificant viewer of a majestic spectacle.

An enormous uproar now exploded in the surrounding forest. Baboons in panic, perhaps frightened by a hunting leopard, started an ear-splitting concert. A Scops owl made his monotonous cry immediately above me and the thousands of cicadas, crickets and nocturnal insects shared in the turmoil. Suddenly the elephants were gone without a trace, without a sound. I couldn't believe it. A slowly increasing humming explained the reason. Bumping along, our Land-Rover entered the campsite, making much too much noise for my liking.

Peter was full of excuses. First of all the man of the pumping station was absent, but there was his remote cousin, who lived in Marsabit, but the sister of that cousin had just had a baby – in short, he was sure Bwana Mkubwa would understand.

He did … the smell of *pombe* (native beer) betrayed him, and Ntiso's eyes, although small, shone and sparkled like stars. When I ordered him to

Between the tusks of the royal Ahmed, the most famous elephant in the world, which was protected, by special decree, by President Kenyatta. In the wild to stand like this is almost certainly to commit suicide. Ahmed is a very life-like copy made of glass fibre and stuffed by expert taxidermists. He now adorns the National Museum of Kenya's capital, Nairobi. The value of the tusks is estimated at 500,000 Belgian francs ($ 17,000)

provide a meal *pesi-pesi*, he tiptoed off to his improvised kitchen – two stones and a grid – muttering : '*Chakula tiari, Bwana Mzee CHAKULA TYARI UPESI !'* (The food will be ready in a minute !)

To Peter, who was standing at a peculiar angle, I related briefly the visit of Ahmed. Hoping for enthusiasm, I was rather taken aback when he exclaimed with his pink palms held up, '*Satani ya kibrani*' – the devil of the forest ! – as if he was pleased to have escaped this misfortune. Rather annoyed, I curtly told him : '*lete beer moja upesi*' – bring me a beer, quickly ! With raised eyebrows he picked up the bottle beside my chair, and held it up against the light from the now high flames of the camp-fire and pointed out that in my excitement I had not yet touched it ...

The next morning, before sunrise, I woke up Peter to go and visit King Ahmed. We cut through the forest in all directions, and investigated all possible valleys. That night I returned to my folding chair, ordered total silence and forbade the lighting of the fire. At the original place no single buffalo or elephant returned for a drink. Yet, I did spot them drinking at the other side of the lake ... but no Ahmed at all, all the time we camped at Sokorte Dika or Lake Paradise. The game scouts of John Alexander came to tell us that they, too, had observed Ahmed near their camp. When we reached it, he had vanished. The next day there was a heavy downpour, the following day, a dense fog. Never again would I see a glimpse of the legendary Ahmed.

Hundreds of storks came to the lake by day, and in the afternoon as they flew higher and higher in wide circles on the hot-air currents they gave me many an exciting moment. I recorded the large kudu-antelope, baboons, water birds, all sorts of animals, even the black cuckoo. I enjoyed myself immensely in this last area of unspoilt wild nature, but there was no trace of Ahmed. With a heavy heart, I left the land of the king of the elephants, promising myself to return the following year. In that year I heard if his death. Since 1956 Ahmed had been spotted by the District Commissioner of Marsabit, 'Windy Wilde'. At that time another big boss inhabited Marsabit, tembo 'Mohammed' with his longest tusk measuring 11 feet (3.40 metres) long. The fourth on the world's record list, he died a natural death in 1956.

Ahmed died in 1974, when he was fifty-five years old. Stuffed by taxidermists, he now decorates the national museum in Nairobi with the plate;

UNDER THE HIGH PROTECTION OF PRESIDENT KENYATTA.

Nobody lives for ever. On 22nd Auogust 1978, during my safari in the Masai-Mara region, Tor Allan, my companion who, with his field radio, had each evening contacted Nairobi, heard that Mzee, the president who had granted Ahmed his protective decree, had died.

The last of an endagered species, the rare Grevy's zebra, resident of northern Kenya, Ethiopia, and Somalia. It is able to eat grass that is too coarse and tough for most other grazers. Heavily poached and now more difficult to see than they were even a few years ago.
Isiolo range. Chrismas 1979.

The vast and endless Keedong vally. Southern Kenya.

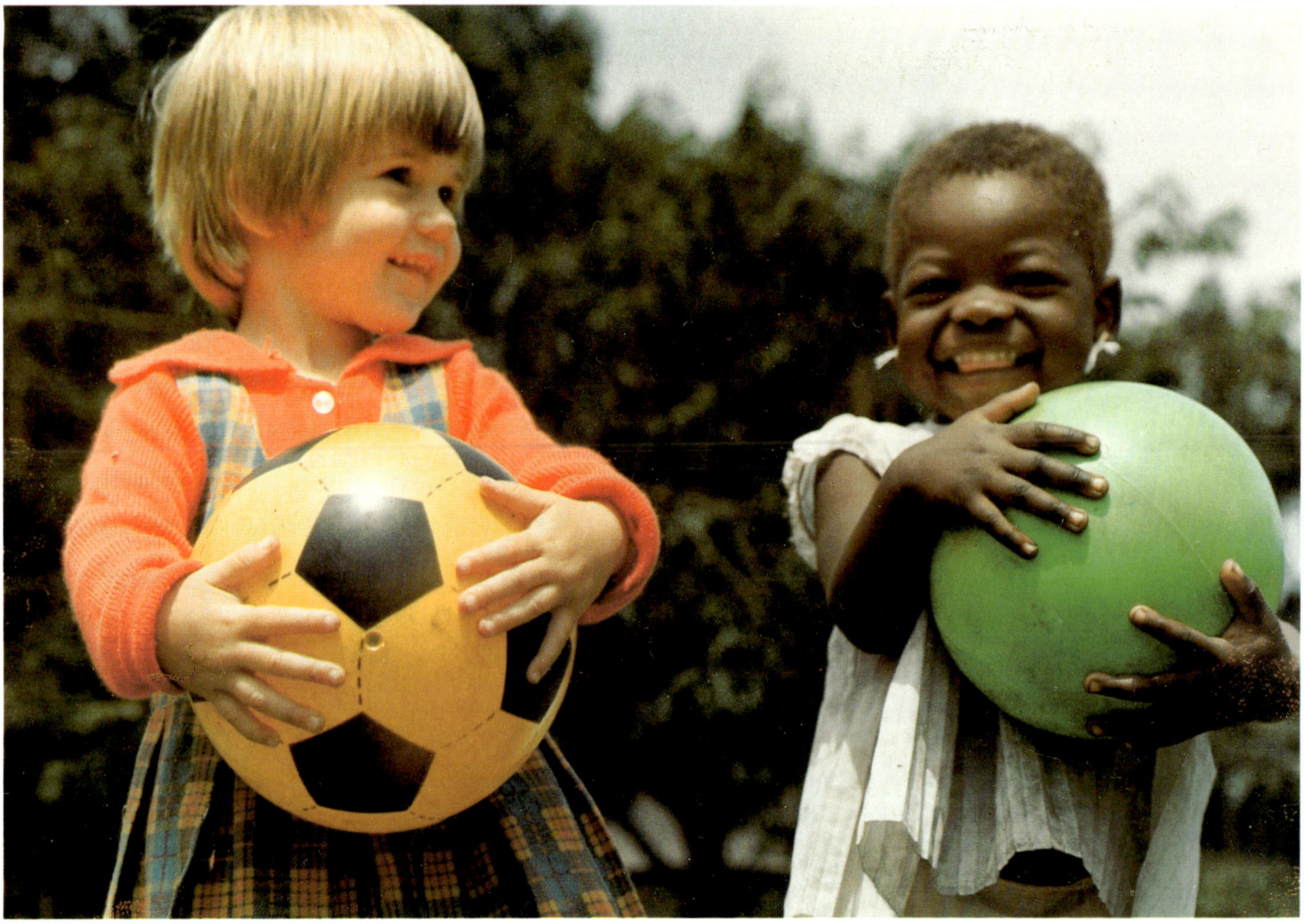

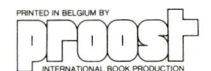

Epilogue

This book will be published in England shortly after the Year of the Child. In East Africa that was the 'International anti-apartheid year'. Let us hope that the human race, at the top of the evolutionary scale and at present amounting to four milliards – a number which will have doubled by the turn of the century – will become aware of the undescribable slaughter which has caused more animal species to be exterminated in the last two hundred years than had ever been thought possible – and that it must come to an end. Man should realise that the animal kingdom is part of his cultural pattern, in which he could perhaps act as regulator, but under no circumstances as total master or exterminator. It would be sad if our descendants, living in their plastic, glass and cement boxes, impressed by ever-advancing technology, spending vast sums of money on collecting stone grit and sulphuric acid from remote planets, and even more money on atom and neutron bombs, could see only films and photographs of what once was our heritage, our most precious inheritance, the fauna and flora of this world – our world.

PRINTED IN BELGIUM BY
proost
INTERNATIONAL BOOK PRODUCTION

NEW ENGLISH LIBRARY
TIMES MIRROR

First published in 1980 by New English Library Ltd.
Designer: DPC - Helmond (Holland)
Author: Marc Sleen (Belgium)
Printed in Belgium by Henri Proost & Cie, Turnhout

All correspondence concerning the contents of this volume should be addressed to Proost
International Book Production, Everdongenlaan 23 B - 2300 Turnhout

ISBN 0 450 04445 9
Printed in Belgium